# ELDON WEISHEIT

## Visual Messages on Old Testament Texts Series A

**AUGSBURG** Publishing House • Minneapolis

*Dedicated to Carolyn*
*on our 25th wedding anniversary*

GOD'S PROMISE FOR CHILDREN — SERIES A

Copyright © 1980 Augsburg Publishing House

Library of Congress Catalog Card No. 80-65554

International Standard Book No. 0-8066-1799-3

MANUFACTURED IN THE UNITED STATES OF AMERICA

# Contents

Preface .......................................................................... 6

Pick a Winner (Isaiah 2:2-3a) ................................... 8

Jesus Comes Between You and Others
(Isaiah 11:5-6a) ................................................. 10

Don't Throw It Away! (Isaiah 35:4-6a) ................... 12

Watch for the Right Sign (Isaiah 7:14) .................... 14

What'll We Name the Baby? (Isaiah 9:6) ................ 16

God and You Gave Real Gifts (Isaiah 63:8-9a) ........ 18

Use His Name to Bless (Numbers 6:27) ................... 20

Christmas Is Only the Beginning (Isaiah 61:11) ...... 22

Look What Others See in You (Isaiah 60:1-3) .......... 24

God Gives You the Right Clue (Isaiah 42:1a) .......... 26

Jesus Does the Whole Job (Isaiah 49:6) .................... 28

You Have Seen the Light (Isaiah 9:2-3a) ................... 30

What Shall I Give to God? (Micah 6:6, 8) .............. 32

Don't Give God Leftovers (Isaiah 58:5-7) ................ 34

You Have a Choice (Deuteronomy 30:19-20) .......... 36

So Who Wants to Be Even? (Leviticus 19:17-18) .... 38

God Will Never Forget You (Isaiah 49:16) ............ 40

Two Gifts on the Mountain (Exodus 24:12) ............ 42

Who Is Telling the Truth? (Genesis 3:4-5) .............. 44

God Is with You on Every Step (Genesis 12:1-3) .... 46

Be Led by God's Eyes (Isaiah 42:16) ........................ 48

When Will You Ask for Help? (Hosea 5:15) .......... 50

New Life from Dry Bones (Ezekiel 37:3, 11, 14a) .. 52

What Does God Have to Say Today? (Isaiah 50:4) .. 54

A Savior to Be Seen (Acts 10:40-41) ........................ 56

Don't Quit Halfway Through (Acts 2:23-24) .......... 58

Look at God's Menu (Acts 2:38-39) ........................ 60

When God Talks, Listen! (Acts 7:51) ........................ 62

A Way to Be Open-Minded (Acts 17:11) ................ 64

Find What You Already Have (Acts 17:23) ............ 66

God's Delivery System (Acts 1:8) ............................ 68

God Pours His Spirit on You (Joel 2:28-29) ............ 70

Search the Past (Deuteronomy 4:32) ........................ 72

God Gives You a Choice (Deuteronomy 11:26-28) .. 74

Love That Lasts (Hosea 6:4, 6) ................................ 76

Watch What Deal You Accept (Exodus 19:5a, 8) .... 78

Think Before You Quit (Jeremiah 20:7, 9) .............. 80

Which Prophet Will You Believe?
  (Jeremiah 28:8-9) ................................................ 82

How Do I Know for Sure? (Zechariah 9:11) ............ 84

The Word in the World (Isaiah 55:10-11) .............. 86

God Has a Purpose (Isaiah 44:7a) ............................ 88

Ask God to Help You Help Yourself
  (1 Kings 3:10-12) ................................................ 90

Buy Without Money (Isaiah 55:1) ............................ 92

You Are Not Alone (1 Kings 19:14b, 18) ................ 94

One Size Fits All (Isaiah 56:7b) ............................ 96

God by Another Name Is Lord (Exodus 6:2-3) ........ 98

Forgiveness for One—and All
(Jeremiah 15:15a, 19a) ........................................ 100

Pass the Message On (Ezekiel 38:8-9) ...................... 102

Good Can Come from Evil (Genesis 50:19-20) ........ 104

Our Way and God's Way (Isaiah 55:8-9) ................ 106

The Right Way and the Wrong Way
(Ezekiel 18:25, 31-32) ........................................ 108

What Does God Expect of You? (Isaiah 5:7) ............ 110

When Do You Say "Thanks God"? (Isaiah 25:8-9) .. 112

One Person's Blessing—Another's Disaster
(Isaiah 45:7) ........................................................ 114

Give Love—Not Revenge (Leviticus 19:18) ............ 116

Don't Be Scared Any More (Amos 5:18-19a) .......... 118

Keep the Name Tags Straight (Hosea 11:3-4) .......... 120

Help Me Be a Good Teacher (Malachi 2:6) ............ 122

Read the Instructions, Before You Fail
(Jeremiah 26:4b-5) .............................................. 124

Christ Has Two Jobs (Ezekiel 34:23) ...................... 126

# Preface

Object lessons are as old as the Old Testament.

Early in the history of the world God used the rainbow as a visual reminder of the covenant he made with all people. Both the covenant and the object that reminds us of God's promise are still in effect.

Moses put a bronze snake on a pole—the object of the lesson was repentance. Jeremiah hid his linen shorts under a rock, he broke a clay jar—both to illustrate a message from God.

The Old Testament is filled with visual messages for people who rarely had a copy of the sacred writings to read but who heard them regularly. When they thought of the message from God their minds did not see words but pictures and actions. The message from God was seen in great miracles, exciting drama, and the everyday events of a potter working with clay, shepherds caring for their sheep, a farmer threshing grain.

The object lessons in this book are not an attempt to re-enact the events of the Old Testament or to reuse the objects used by the prophets to illustrate their messages. The objects used in this book are from today's world to show that the events of the Old Testament are also for today's world.

As children grow in the faith and understanding of the Gospel of Jesus Christ they need the rich resources of spiritual power available in the Old Testament. These sermons are to help kids develop roots that reach back to the ancient promises of God.

Most of these sermons have been preached as a part of

the regular Sunday worship at Fountain of Life Lutheran Church in Tucson, Arizona. They were used either as presented here, as a children's sermon, or as part of the regular sermon.

The sermons for kids are shared with you with the hope that they may add to the joy and effectiveness of your ministry as they have to mine. I find another blessing from the children's sermons that I hope you may also share—may they add to the depth and fun of the relationship between you, the children in your congregation or classroom, and your Savior.

ELDON WEISHEIT

# Pick a Winner

**THE WORD:**

In days to come the mountain where the Temple stands will be the highest one of all, towering above all the hills. Many nations will come streaming to it, and their people will say, "Let us go up the hill of the Lord, to the Temple of Israel's God. He will teach us what he wants us to do."

Isaiah 2:2-3a (First Sunday in Advent)

**THE WORLD:**

A picture of each: A new racing car, an old car, a nationally known politician, an unknown person, an army, the baby Jesus in the manger.

I want to see how good you are at picking winners. First, let's see which of these two cars you'd pick to win a race. *(Show cars.)* One is a sleek race car, the other a clunker. That's easy, the race car would win.

Now let's see if you can pick a winner in an election. You recognize this person *(famous politician)?* This is _____. Now suppose he were running against this person *(unknown)* in an election. Who do you think would win? That's easy. The one that was well known would win.

One more: Which is more powerful—this army, or this baby? The answer looks easy. Any army is more powerful than a baby. We always pick a winner by choosing the one that has the most—the most money, the most fame, the most power. A baby has none of those things.

But before you choose the army as the winner, you had better look at the baby again. This is not just any old baby. This is the one born in Bethlehem almost 2000 years ago. Soldiers from an army tried to kill him right after he was born. But he escaped. Later he was killed by members of an army. But he came back to life after he had been buried for three days.

This is Jesus—the Savior of the world. Countless armies have come and gone, won and lost since his birth. But Jesus is still the Savior of the world. If you want to pick a winner, pick him—the baby from Bethlehem.

Many years before Jesus was born Isaiah told people that something special was going to take place. In our Bible reading he said all nations would come to the temple. There they would meet the God of Israel and he would teach them. God sent Jesus to that temple to teach all people about God's love and forgiveness.

At the time of Isaiah the nation of Israel, its temple and its God looked like losers. Babylon looked much more like a winner. In fact, later the army from Babylon wiped out Israel and carried the people off as slaves.

Yet Isaiah was right. The God of Israel was the winner. His message of salvation now includes all people. We are preparing to celebrate the birth of Jesus again. Since his life on earth Jesus has changed many lives. The people who follow him have become the Christian church. We have large buildings and many people.

But don't pick the Christian church as a winner because of its numbers and its buildings. The Christian church is great only because Jesus has made it what it is. Though we were all sinners and losers, Jesus picked us. Because he is the winner, we will be too.

Each year we celebrate Advent to remind us that our faith is in God who sent his Son to be a baby born in a manger. We don't pick him because he looked like a winner. But he has picked us. Because we are his, we are preparing to celebrate his birth again.

# Jesus Comes
# Between You and Others

**THE WORD:**

He will rule his people with justice and integrity. Wolves and sheep will live together in peace.

Isaiah 11:5-6a (Second Sunday in Advent)

**THE WORLD:**

A fragile Christmas tree ornament, a rock from a collection, a gift box and packing material.

Some things just don't go together. The Bible reading talks about putting a wolf and a sheep together. You know what would happen if a wolf and a sheep were in the same cage at the zoo. The wolf would eat the sheep for dinner.

Or suppose you wanted to give a friend both this rock and this Christmas ornament as a gift. Would you put them in the same box? *(Do it.)* You know what would happen if someone dropped or shook the box. The rock would break the ornament.

Also some people can't be put together. Every time they are together they hurt each other. Are you sometimes like the glass ornament? Are there people who hurt you every time you are with them? Is there someone who calls you names, chases or hits you or laughs at you? When you are with that person you may feel like a sheep in a cage with a wolf, or an ornament in a box with a rock.

But sometimes you may be like the rock. Is there someone that you always hurt? Do you call someone names, hit or chase that person or laugh at him or her? If so, you make that person unhappy. That person feels like a sheep in a cage with a wolf, or a piece of glass in a box with a rock when he or she is with you.

But our Bible reading says that the time will come when the wolf and sheep can live together in peace. People will be able to live together without hurting one another. We will be free from the anger, hatred, jealousy, greed, and all the other things that cause us to hurt each other.

Isaiah tells us that the time of peace will come when the Messiah comes. He says, "He, that is the Messiah, will rule his people with justice and integrity." The Messiah, who is our Savior, will change our lives. He will be fair with us. He will take away our sin. He will give us a new life. He will love each of us and help us love one another.

You can put the rock and the glass ornament in the same box. You can, if you use the right packing material. *(Wrap both the rock and the ornament.)* See when these things are wrapped, they are protected. *(Put them in the box. Shake the box, show the glass again.)* The packing protects the glass from being broken by the rock. It also protects the rock from breaking the glass.

Jesus also comes to protect us from those who hurt us. He loves us; so we know we are okay even if some others do not love us. He helps us forgive those who hurt us; so we don't become filled with anger and hurt ourselves. He helps us understand why others are hateful.

Jesus also comes to protect us from hurting others. He helps us understand how others feel. He gives us love so we can love others even though they are different from us. He forgives us when we have hurt others.

Think of Jesus as the packing material between you and other people. He comes to you, not to separate you from others, but to help you be with others—and for others to be with you. He helps you so you will not hurt others and others will not hurt you.

# Don't Throw It Away!

**THE WORD:**

Tell everyone who is discouraged, "Be strong and don't be afraid! God is coming to your rescue, coming to punish your enemies." The blind will be able to see, and the deaf will hear. The lame will leap and dance, and those who cannot speak will shout for joy.

Isaiah 35:4-6a (Third Sunday in Advent)

**THE WORLD:**

A battery-operated toy (with a battery out so it will not work) that has a written guarantee in or on its package.

---

Are you excited when you receive a present? That's part of the fun of Christmas, isn't it? Suppose you receive this gift. It is a walkie-talkie set. You can use it to talk to a friend who is in another room. You could, that is, if it worked. But look. When I turn the switch on nothing happens. That is a disappointment.

You might feel like throwing the toy away. After all, it doesn't work. What's the use of keeping it? When you see it you will be reminded of your disappointment. But wait. See this guarantee. The company that made the toy also guarantees it. This paper says if the walkie-talkie does not work properly, you can send it back to the company that made it and they will repair it. The people who made it also promise to fix it.

Sometimes we are like that walkie-talkie set. We are not able to do what we are supposed to do. Have you ever felt disappointed in yourself because you couldn't do something you wanted to do? Maybe you didn't get to be on a team or in a choir. Or you didn't make as good a grade as you thought you would. Or you want to be friends with a certain gang of kids, but they don't like you. Or you know your parents are disappointed because you can't do something they want you to do. Or you keep doing the same sin; though you know God said not to do it. Or maybe you don't like the way you look.

What do you do when you are disappointed in yourself? Do you give up? Do you say, "I'm no good"? Do you throw your life away? No. Remember the toy had a guarantee. The people who made it promised to fix it. You also have a guarantee. The God who made you promised to take care of you. He promises to fix your life.

Listen to the guarantee. Isaiah wrote it in our Bible reading, "Tell everyone who is discouraged, 'Be strong and don't be afraid! God is coming to your rescue, coming to punish your enemies.' The blind will be able to see, the deaf will hear. The lame will leap and dance and those who cannot speak will shout for joy."

God made this promise a long time ago. He promised he would come to help the people he had created. He kept that promise when Jesus was born. Jesus came to help people. He made the blind see and the deaf hear. He helped the lame walk. He gave comfort and help to all people. He forgave all sins. He opened the way for all people to go to heaven with him.

Jesus is still with us today. We are getting ready to celebrate his birth again. We celebrate it every year so we can remember how God kept his promise to come and help us. You may still have problems. But don't throw your life away. Remember the guarantee. God said to tell those who are discouraged, "Be strong and don't be afraid. I am coming to your rescue."

# Watch for the Right Sign

**THE WORD:**

Isaiah said to Ahaz, "Well then, the Lord himself will give you a sign: a young woman who is pregnant will have a son and will name him 'Immanuel.'"

Isaiah 7:14 (Fourth Sunday in Advent)

**THE WORLD:**

Signs made to look like house numbers with the following: 1416, 1420, 1424, 1428, 1432.

Suppose you are going to visit a friend who lives at 1424 Spring Street. You find Spring Street and the first house you see has this number: 1416. The next house has this number: 1420. You know you are going the right direction because the numbers are going higher. But sometimes it is difficult to see the numbers on a house. And some houses are back from the road where no one can see them. So the next house you see has this number: 1428. Remember you are looking for 1424. When you came to 1428 you know you have gone too far. If you keep going you will come to this number: 1432. Instead you turn around and go back until you come to the house between 1420 and 1428. That's where your friend lives.

In the Old Testament God gave King Ahaz of Judah a sign. The sign showed the people how God planned to help them. This was the sign: "A young woman who is pregnant will have a son and will call him 'Immanuel.'"

God's sign to Judah said a special baby was coming. Many babies are born—just as many houses are on Spring Street. So watching for new babies was like finding the right street. The help was to come from a baby. But not just any baby. The sign was a baby who was to be born who would be called "Immanuel." Immanuel is not just a name like our names: Karen, Kevin, Todd, Joan. The word Immanuel means God with us. God would send a special baby who would be called "God with us."

For years the people of Judah watched for this special baby. They were looking ahead to his birth. They were like someone who saw 1416 and 1420 when they were looking for the house numbered 1424. They knew the time for the baby to be born was getting closer. And the baby was born in Bethlehem—almost 2000 years ago. A baby who by his life showed that he was "God with us." He was called the names that are used for God. He accepted worship that is only for God. The power of God was at work in him.

Today we are like people walking down the street the other way. We also are looking for the baby. We come to 1432, 1428, and the next number is 1424. That's what we are looking for. We look back into history to the birth of a baby that was called "God with us."

We cannot count all the babies who have been born since God first gave this sign to King Ahaz of Judah. But of all those babies only one has been "God with us." Only one has brought the power and love of God to earth to be a part of us. Only one baby grew up to be the Savior who gave himself as a sacrifice for our sins.

This sign that was given to King Ahaz is as important to us as it was to him. The sign showed the king who was coming. It shows us who is here.

# What'll We Name the Baby?

**THE WORD:**

A child is born to us! A son is given to us! And he will be
our ruler. He will be called, "Wonderful Counselor,"
"Mighty God," "Eternal Father," "Prince of Peace."

Isaiah 9:6 (Christmas Day)

**THE WORLD:**

Stuffed toys (or pictures of) dogs: one all black, one with
spots, one with floppy ears.

See these three dogs. One of them is named Fido. Can
you tell which one is Fido? Any of them could have that
name. Fido is a good name for a dog. You could give a
dog that name even before you saw the dog.

Another one of these dogs is Spot. Which one do you
think is Spot? This is easy, isn't it? Whoever named this
dog Spot had seen the dog. His name describes what he is.
And guess what this dog (the black one) is named? Right
—he is called Blackie. That means this one must be Fido.
But if he had been named after you saw him, his name
might have been Floppy.

Most of our names do not describe us. By your name I
can tell if you are a boy or girl, but I don't know much
else about you until I know you. Our nicknames often
tell more about us. People give us nicknames as we grow
older. These names tell something about us. Can you see
the person who is called: Red, Lefty, Freckles, Smiley,
Shortie?

Today we are here to celebrate the birth of a baby. His
parents named him Jesus because an angel had told them
to. The name, Jesus, describes the baby. It means Savior.

16

Jesus is the Savior of the world. But other Jewish babies were also named Jesus. Many parents were waiting for the Messiah; so they named their babies Jesus as a reminder of the promised Savior. Just as today many children are named Christ or Cristina (and in Spanish speaking areas Jesus) as a reminder that we have a Savior.

Jesus also had nicknames. The prophet Isaiah knew what the Messiah would be like. Later, when people believed Jesus to be the Messiah they used Isaiah's words to describe him.

Listen to what our Bible reading says: A child is born to us! A son is given to us! And he will be our ruler. He will be called, "Wonderful Counselor," "Mighty God," "Eternal Father," "Prince of Peace."

One of us would have to live a long time and work hard to be called Wonderful Counselor. But Isaiah knew that the Messiah would be a wonderful Counselor—one who would direct our lives. Isaiah also knew that this Messiah would be the Almighty God living with us. He would be able to say, "The Father and I are one," so he can be called the Eternal Father. He would be the Prince of Peace who would give peace to us because he forgives our sins and helps us live at peace with one another and with God.

What will you call the baby—the one born long ago in the manger? When you see him you know what he is like. Then you can call him by names that describe what he is for you.

# God and You Gave Real Gifts

**THE WORD:**

The Lord said, "They are my people; they will not deceive me." And so he saved them from all their suffering. It was not an angel, but the Lord himself who saved them.

Isaiah 63:8-9a (First Sunday after Christmas)

**THE WORLD:**

An empty box wrapped as a Christmas gift, an angel and the Christ child from a nativity set.

Did you give a Christmas present to God? Though we can give gifts to God, we can't give him a wrapped package like we give to our family and friends. But let's pretend this package is your gift to God. It's a nice-looking package. If God had a Christmas tree, this gift would look good under it. Now, let's open the package. See, it is empty. You wouldn't give an empty package to God, would you?

God knows you wouldn't try to fool him. In our Bible reading for today the Lord says, "They are my people; they will not deceive me." God knows who we are. We are his people. He created us. He loves us. He takes care of us. Since he knows us, we do not deceive him—even if we try. We can't fool him by pretending we are good any more than we could fool him with a fancily wrapped empty box.

The real gift from you to God is yourself. You give yourself to God when you worship him and when you serve him. You give yourself to him when you follow him and love his people. You don't deceive God by pretending to worship and serve him. He knows what is in your heart.

He can see through the wrappings you put around yourself. He knows what is on the inside.

Because God knows everything about us, some people are afraid to give themselves to God. We know we have failed him. We know we have done wrong. We might think it is better to give God an empty package than one filled with our sin. But we don't have to be afraid to give ourselves to God. The Bible reading tells us that he has saved us. God has come to be our Savior. We do not have to suffer for our sin. We do not have to hide our sins. Instead we can give our total selves to God. He will forgive all that is wrong. He will bless all that is good.

We can be free to give ourselves to God because he first gave himself to us. Our Bible reading also says, "It was not an angel, but the Lord himself who saved them." Think of the Christmas story again. Remember the angels *(show angel)*. The angels told Mary and Joseph that Christ would be born. The angels sang his praises to the shepherds. But God did not send the angels to save us. They only told us the message.

God sent his Son to save us *(show the baby)*. Christmas shows us how God gave himself to us by becoming one of us. God didn't send someone else to do the job. He came himself to be our Savior.

Because God gave you a real gift when he gave you himself; you can give God a real gift when you give him yourself. Don't be afraid to go to him as you are. He has come to you to change you to be like him.

# Use His Name to Bless

**THE WORD:**

And the Lord said, "If they pronounce my name as a blessing upon the people of Israel, I will bless them."

Numbers 6:27 (The Name of Jesus)

**THE WORLD:**

A bowl of sugar, a filled saltshaker, Koolaid, glass of water, and a spoon.

Eric was mad at his sister Cindy. He knew she liked to make Koolaid; so he dumped the sugar out of its bowl and put salt in its place. *(Do it.)* He laughed when he thought how Cindy would look when she drank the Koolaid made with salt instead of sugar.

Later Cindy made a glass of Koolaid. *(Do it.)* She took a sip and it tasted terrible. So she put it in the refrigerator. Later Eric came in from playing. He was thirsty. He saw the glass of Koolaid; so he grabbed it and took a big drink. It was awful. Eric intended to pull a trick on Cindy. But it backfired on him.

Let's use the story about Eric and Cindy to understand something about how we use God's name. Today we celebrate the day the baby who was born in the stable was named. His parents called him Jesus as the angel had told them to. In our Bible reading God promises, "If they pronounce my name as a blessing upon the people of Israel, I will bless them." Think of all the names we call God: Father, Jehovah, Creator, Lord, and others. Each name tells us something about the great things God is doing for us.

Think of his name as being like the sugar in the story.

The sugar was intended to make Cindy's drink taste good. God's name is intended to be a blessing for us. We are blessed when we hear how God has created us and takes care of us. We are blessed when we know that Jesus is our Savior—that he takes away our sin and gives us eternal life. We are blessed when we know that the Holy Spirit gives us faith and keeps us close to God.

But sometimes people use God's name in other ways. Instead of blessing with his name, they curse. Instead of using God's name to love and help others, they use the holy name to hate and hurt. That is like Eric putting salt in the sugar bowl. He wanted to cause a problem for someone else.

When we use God's name to hurt someone else, we are also hurting ourselves. Remember Cindy only took a sip of the salty drink. Eric took a big gulp. If you use God's name to curse you hurt another person. But you hurt yourself even more. You show a lack of love and respect for God.

However, if you use God's name to bless others, you not only bless them, but you also receive a blessing for yourself. It is good that we start the New Year on the day Jesus was named. It is a reminder for us to use his name as a blessing all year.

Remember the promise God gave you. If someone else blesses you with God's name, God will also bless you. If you bless someone else with God's name, God will bless the other person—and you too.

# Christmas Is Only the Beginning

**THE WORD:**

> As surely as seeds sprout and grow, the Sovereign Lord will save his people, and all the nations will praise him.
> Isaiah 61:11 (Second Sunday after Christmas)

**THE WORLD:**

> An orange and a seed from another orange, the manger and baby from a nativity set, a crucifix.

---

Christmas is an exciting time, but Christmas is only the beginning. We have heard the story of Joseph and Mary, shepherds and wise men. We have sung the song of the angels. But all of those things are important only because they help us understand how God became one of us when Jesus was born. All of the story is about this *(show the manger and baby)*. We are happy because this baby was born.

And the baby was born for a reason. Our Bible reading for today compares that reason to the planting of a seed. It says, "As surely as seeds sprout and grow, the Sovereign Lord will save his people, and all the nations will praise him."

See this seed. It is small and you might not recognize it. But for generations seeds like this have been planted. The seeds sprouted and grew to be trees. And the trees produced fruit like this orange. People all over the world plant seeds of all kinds. But they don't plant the seeds just for the fun of digging in the dirt. They plant the seeds because seeds sprout and grow. When the seeds grow they produce food for people to eat.

Isaiah says that just as surely as a seed will sprout and

grow, the Sovereign Lord will save his people. When Jesus was born as the baby of Bethlehem, he was like a seed planted by God. The baby was the seed of God's presence planted among people. He grew up among us. He produced fruit—not food for our bodies but food to save our souls. The baby that started his life in a manger became the Savior whose life ended on a cross *(show the crucifix)*. Just as the seed sprouts and grows to produce the orange, the baby grew, lived for us and went to the cross to die in our place so we can be saved.

Christmas is only the beginning of the story. The birth of Jesus is important because it shows us God came to be with us. But his coming is important because of what he did after he was here.

There is another step after the seed sprouts and grows into the tree that produces fruit. We have this fruit so we can eat it. *(Peel the orange. If practical give each child a section. If not, eat a piece of it yourself.)* The fruit grows to be eaten.

Our Bible reading says not only that the Lord will save us, but also, "And all the nations will praise him." Christmas is the beginning of the story. But the story continues and Jesus dies for us. But that is not the end of the story. Jesus comes back from the dead. He lives with us today. We praise him. We praise him for all that he has done. For his birth, his death, his resurrection from the dead, for his being with us now and promising that we can be with him forever.

# Look What Others See in You

**THE WORD:**

> Arise, Jerusalem, and shine like the sun; the glory of the Lord is shining on you! Other nations will be covered by darkness, but on you the light of the Lord will shine; the brightness of his presence will be with you. Nations will be drawn to your light, and kings to the dawning of your new day.
>
> Isaiah 60:1-3 (The Epiphany of Our Lord)

**THE WORLD:**

A screen, slide projector, and picture of Jesus to be projected. (If not available, a cross to cast a shadow on the screen can be used.)

Look at the screen and tell me what you see. First, what do you see now? *(Discuss: The screen is blank, plain white.)* Now what do you see? *(Project the picture of Christ or the cross on the screen.)* Now you see a picture. Tell me about it. *(Talk briefly about the meaning of Christ as the Savior who came to the world to live with us.)*

You see the picture on the screen. Everyone agrees there is a picture of Christ on that screen. But *(turn the projector off)* where is the picture now? The picture of Christ really isn't on the screen. It is in the projector here. See, here is the picture. But the light from the projector shines through the pictures and lets us see the picture over there on the screen.

In our Bible reading for today Isaiah, an Old Testament prophet, told the people who lived a long time ago to be like this screen. He says, "Arise, Jerusalem, and shine like the sun; the glory of the Lord is shining on you!" Jerusalem is the name of a city. It is a special city that also means the people of God. God told the people that he wanted to shine his glory on them. When he did, they would shine like the sun.

God kept his promise when Jesus was born. When Jesus Christ comes into our lives the glory of the Lord shines on us. We see God's glory in the way Jesus became a part of us. We see his glory when we receive his love and forgiveness.

Isaiah also tells us that the glory of the Lord will not shine on all people. He says, "Other nations will be covered by darkness, but on you the light of the Lord will shine; the brightness of his presence will be with you." God's love is for everyone. But not everyone will receive it. Some will hide from him. Some will turn away so the light of God's love cannot shine on them. But they can still see the light if they see God's love at work in us. The Bible reading also says, "Nations will be drawn to your light, and kings to the dawning of your new day."

When the light of God shines on us we receive all the blessings that he has to offer us. Others who do not yet see God can at least see the blessings of love, joy and peace that God gives us. Then they can come to see what God is ready to give them too.

# God Gives You the Right Clue

**THE WORD:**

The Lord says, "Here is my servant, whom I strengthen—the one I have chosen, with whom I am pleased."

Isaiah 42:1a (First Sunday after the Epiphany)

**THE WORLD:**

Six cards (heavy paper at least 5 x 8) each a different color and numbered 1 through 6 with 3 on white or gray.

I need someone to play a game with me. Okay, Cindy, see these cards. They are numbered 1 through 6. *(Show back side of the cards.)* I want you to pick number 3. *(Let her choose a card, identify the number and put it back. Continue until she chooses the right one.)* Okay, Cindy, it took you _____ times to find the right one. The grey card is number 3.

Alan, will you play the game now? See if you can find number 3. Look, Alan got the right card the first time. Let's have someone else do it. *(Have one or two more play —always asking for number 3.)*

It took Cindy _____ times to get the right card. But the rest always got it on the first try. Of course you know why. Cindy had to guess until she found the right one. Then all of you saw the 3 was on the grey card. You now know the right clue to find the right number.

God has also given us a clue to help us know the Savior. He had promised he would come to be a person like us; so he could save us from our sins. But there are lots of people. How do we know which is the right one? Our Bible reading from the prophet Isaiah gives us a clue. God says, "Here is my servant, whom I strengthen—the

26

one I have chosen, with whom I am pleased." He says he will choose the One to be the servant who will save us. And he will be pleased with the servant. All of the other people are sinners. He still loves us. He wants us. But the special servant is different—God is pleased with him. If we are to know who the Savior is, we must find the one with whom God is pleased.

I'll tell you where to look. Look in Matthew Chapter 3 where you can read how Jesus was baptized. After the baptism a voice from heaven said, "This is my own dear Son, with whom I am pleased."

God has given us the clue. He told us to watch for the one with whom he is pleased. But we don't have to guess in order to find that one—like Cindy had to guess until she found the right card. When we hear what God said when Jesus was baptized, we are like Alan. We have the right clue. We know who came to be our Savior. It is Jesus who was born of Mary, died on the cross and rose from the dead.

The clue God gave us not only helps us recognize Jesus when we study the Bible and see what he did long ago. It also helps us recognize Jesus today. Jesus is still the one with whom God is pleased. Jesus is still the servant God chose to save us. Jesus still lives with us. He was baptized and we are baptized in his name. Because God is pleased with Jesus, he is also pleased with us. He can be pleased with us because Jesus has taken away our sin.

God has given us the right clue. Look for the one God is pleased with and God will be pleased with you too.

# Jesus Does the Whole Job

**THE WORD:**
> The Lord said to me, "I have a greater task for you, my servant. Not only will you restore to greatness the people of Israel who have survived, but I will also make you a light to the nations—so that all the world may be saved."
> Isaiah 49:6 (Second Sunday after the Epiphany)

**THE WORLD:**
> A dart game with 4 darts.

Let's suppose you got this dart game for Christmas. When you play with it one dart misses the board and goes behind some furniture. You can't find it. But you can play with three darts. The feathers fall off another—I don't want to ruin this dart but you can pretend the feathers are gone—so you can't use this one. Another is lost when you pack the Christmas decorations away. Now you have one dart. But you can still play.

Then you break the point on the last dart. Now you might as well throw away the dartboard. But you like darts; so you ask your dad if he can fix the last one. He sharpens the broken point. Now you have your dart back. Your dad also fixes the feathers on this one and finds the two you had lost. Now you have all of them back. You can play darts again.

The story of the darts is a parable about God and his people. God created all people. He loves everyone and wants everyone to be with him. But people left him. They were lost and broken—like the darts. When they were gone God might as well have destroyed the world, just as you thought about throwing away the dartboard when the darts were all broken or lost.

Instead of throwing away the world, God sent someone to fix it. Our Bible reading for today tells how God made plans for a Savior to come to the world. God told the Savior, "I have a greater task for you, my servant. Not only will you restore to greatness the people of Israel who have survived, but I will also make you a light to all nations—so that all the world may be saved."

God sent Jesus to find all who were lost and to fix all who were broken. God used this promise to remind us that the Savior would come for all people. Now the Savior has come. We thank God that Jesus came for everyone —for the people in China, and Africa, and the people next door. And those in your class at school. He came to save everyone.

When God sent Jesus to save us, Jesus came for all people. Jesus did the whole job. You can know he is your Savior because he also saved others. You can know he saves others because he has saved you.

# You Have Seen the Light

**THE WORD:**

The people who walked in darkness have seen a great light. They lived in a land of shadows, but now light is shining on them. You have given them great joy, Lord; you have made them happy.

Isaiah 9:2-3a (Third Sunday after the Epiphany)

**THE WORLD:**

An apple hidden in the area of the speaker.

---

You know what it is like to be in the dark, don't you? Even if we turned out the lights, this room wouldn't be dark now. But imagine you were here at night and the lights were out. If you tried to walk through the church at night you would run into a pew, trip over a step and bang your head on the altar. But if you turned on the light it would be easy to walk through the church—even at night.

Sometimes we say we are "in the dark" even when we can see. Being "in the dark" means we don't know something. For example, you are near an apple right now. Some of you are only two feet away from the apple. But you can't see it. If I asked you to look for the apple you would stumble around in all directions. You would be in the dark.

The apple is *(tell where it is)*. Since I've told you where it is you are no longer in the dark. See. Here it is. *(Show it.)* When I put the apple back *(do it)*, you can't see it, but you're not in the dark anymore. You know where it is. You could walk right to it.

Our Bible reading talks about people who walked in darkness. It doesn't mean they were taking a hike at night.

Even in the day time, they were "in the dark." They were lost from God. They had turned away from God and couldn't see him any more. Even though God still loved them and took care of them, they could not see him. They were people in the dark. They didn't know where to look for God. They stumbled through life because they didn't know where they were going.

However the Bible reading says, " . . . but now light is shining on them. You have given them great joy, Lord." God sent a light to the people. First the light was a promise to send the Savior. Before the Savior came the promise was a light to the people—just as when I told you where the apple was before I showed it to you.

You and I live after the Savior has come. We have not only the promise from our Bible reading, but we also have the Savior. Jesus has come to be with us. He tells us that if we have seen him we have seen God. He is the light that shows us the way to live with God.

Sometimes we still feel as though we are in darkness. We stumble around through life. We make mistakes. We do wrong. We hurt ourselves and others. When that happens to you remember this promise from God, "The people who walked in darkness have seen a great light." Jesus is your great light. He forgives the wrong you have done. He heals you when you hurt yourself. He loves you and shows you the way to be with God now and forever.

# What Shall I Give to God?

**THE WORD:**
> What shall I bring to the Lord, the God of heaven, when I come to worship him? Shall I bring the best calves to burn as offerings to him? No, the Lord has told us what is good. What he requires of us is this: to do what is just, to show constant love, and to live in humble fellowship with our God.
>
> Micah 6:6, 8 (Fourth Sunday after the Epiphany)

**THE WORLD:**
> Flowers (perhaps from the altar), a toy, coins.

Sometimes people give gifts when they visit family or friends. If you go stay at someone's house, you might take a gift. If they come to visit you they might bring a gift to you.

Others would know who you were visiting by the gift you took. Suppose you were taking this gift *(the flowers)*. Who would you be visiting? Maybe someone in the hospital, or your grandmother. What if you were taking this gift *(the toy)?* Then you are going to visit a child.

Today you have come to see God. Did you bring him a gift? Our Bible reading asks you to think about a present for God. It says, "What shall I bring to the Lord, the God of heaven, when I come to worship him? Shall I bring the best calves to burn as offerings to him?"

The prophet Micah wrote these words a long time ago when people burned animals as sacrifices. He thought he would take some calves as a gift to God. Today we use money as our offerings. Perhaps you brought some of your allowance as an offering to God. You may have a dime or a quarter or a dollar to give. Money seems like a good gift to God. God has blessed you so you have money to give. Therefore you give some back to him; just as God has given calves to people in Micah's day so they gave calves to God.

But listen to what else Micah says. After asking if he should give calves, he writes, "No, the Lord has told us what is good. What he requires of us is this: to do what is just, to show constant love, and to live in humble fellowship with our God."

God had given the people of the Old Testament much more than calves. He had loved them. He had taken care of them. He had often rescued them from danger and saved them. So Micah said their gift should reflect what God had done for them. They should love God and the people he loves. They should be fair and honest. Their gift to God should include obedience to his will.

We can and should give money as part of our worship to God. But remember God has given us more than money. Look at the gift God has given you. He gave you his Son, Jesus Christ. Jesus lived for you, died for you, and came back to life again. Through him you also will live forever.

The gift you bring to God today is not just your money —it is yourself. God gave himself to you. You can give yourself to God. When you give yourself to God, I will not put you on the altar as a burned sacrifice. Your gift of yourself to God is a living sacrifice, not a burned one. You can live for him by loving other people as he has loved you, by forgiving others as he has forgiven you, by serving others as he has served you.

# Don't Give God Leftovers

**THE WORD:**

When you fast, you make yourselves suffer; you bow your heads low like a blade of grass and spread out sackcloth and ashes to lie on. Is that what you call fasting? Do you think I will be pleased with that? The kind of fasting I want is this: Remove the chains of oppression and yoke of injustice, and let the oppressed go free. Share your food with the hungry and open your homes to the homeless poor. Give clothes to those who have nothing to wear, and do not refuse to help your own relatives.

Isaiah 58:5-7 (Fifth Sunday after the Epiphany)

**THE WORLD:**

Two sweaters, one new, the other old and tattered.

---

Suppose a family you know has a boy or girl just your age and size. The family's house burns down. Everything they own is destroyed by the fire. You know they have no clothes to wear. So you and your friends decide to give some clothes to the kids your size. One friend gives shoes, another pants or dress, another a coat. You are to give a sweater.

You go home and find these two sweaters. One is new —you got it for Christmas last year. The other is old— so old and tattered that you were ready to throw it in a rag bag. Which will you give to the kid your size?

Often we give away only what we want to get rid of. Instead we should give what others need. Sometimes we even give God the wrong gifts. In our Bible reading Isaiah says people gave the wrong gifts to God. They fasted, that means they didn't eat. They wore clothes and put ashes on themselves on special days. They made themselves suffer to pay for their own sins.

But God didn't want those kinds of gifts. Instead God wants us to help people in trouble. He wants us to give food to hungry people, clothes to those who need them. God wants us to give gifts to him by giving gifts to others.

You and I probably don't try to please God by going without food or by making ourselves suffer. We know that Jesus has suffered and died in our place. We don't have to punish ourselves for our sins. Christ has taken our punishment for us.

However we can still make the mistake that Isaiah mentioned. We can give God what we want to give rather than what God wants to get. Sometimes we give God only our leftovers—like giving the old sweater. Sometimes we are willing to give only the money we don't need, the time we don't have anything else to do, the things we don't care about.

Don't give God leftovers. God gave you his Son. God gives you first place in his heart. He cares about you. He wants you to love him the way he loves you.

Think of ways you can serve God. Isaiah tells you some things you can do. You can help people. You can stick up for the kid that others laugh at. You can welcome the new kid in school. You can talk to old people. You can be kind to parents, brothers, and sisters. You can share what you have with others who are in need. Then you are giving God what he wants. You'll find you like to give that way; because you're giving back to God the great things he has given you.

# You Have a Choice

**THE WORD:**

I am now giving you the choice between life and death, between God's blessing and God's curse, and I call heaven and earth to witness the choice you make. Choose life. Love the Lord your God, obey him and be faithful to him, and then you and your descendants will live long in the land that he promised to give your ancestors, Abraham, Isaac, and Jacob.

Deuteronomy 30:19-20 (Sixth Sunday after the Epiphany)

**THE WORLD:**

Eight pieces of paper with the following: math homework, pictures from a children's TV program, A, F, Jesus, Me, Life in heaven, Death in hell.

---

I'm going to give you a choice. Would you rather do this homework *(math)* or watch this TV program *(pictures)*? Now I'll give you another choice. Which grade would you rather have on your report card, this *(F)* or this *(A)*?

You do have a choice about which grade you get. But that choice depends on other choices you make. You choose what grade you get when you decide whether to watch TV or do your homework, when you decide to listen in class or talk to a friend. The choice you make each day shows which grade you choose.

In our Bible reading Moses tells us that God gives us a choice. He says we can choose between life *(show paper)* or death *(show paper)*. Which would you choose? Of course, you want to go to heaven. Moses tells you that you are making that choice every day of your life. You choose when you decide if you want to love God, obey him and be faithful to him, or if you want to ignore him, disobey him and serve only yourself.

You have the choice today. You can choose to follow Jesus *(show paper)* or yourself *(show paper)*. Jesus tells you to love people and to speak kind words. Do you hate some people and say unkind words? Jesus tells us to be loving and decent about sex. Do you talk about sex as though it were dirty and nasty? Jesus tells you to keep your word and use his name in love. Do you often break promises and use God's name to curse or swear?

Think about how many times you make a choice between good and evil. You know you often choose to do wrong. By yourself, you have no choice. You are a sinner. You can't help but choose sin.

But God loves you. He gave you his Son to die for your sins and to give you forgiveness. Because God first chose you in Jesus Christ, you now have a choice. You can receive his love; you can be forgiven; you can choose to do good instead of evil.

Moses doesn't want you to wait until judgment day to choose between death and life. Instead he wants you to know now that God has chosen you. Jesus has prepared a place in heaven for you. Because God has chosen you, you can choose to follow him. Each time you have to make a choice between good and evil, think about the choice God has made. Then follow God's choice. Go his way.

# So Who Wants to Be Even?

**THE WORD:**

> God said, "Do not bear a grudge against anyone, but settle your differences with him, so that you will not commit a sin because of him. Do not take revenge on anyone or continue to hate him, but love your neighbor as you love yourself. I am the Lord. Leviticus 19:17-18
> (Seventh Sunday after the Epiphany)

**THE WORLD:**

A graph as shown in diagram. Make the bars of colored paper so they can be shortened or lengthened.

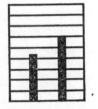

This chart measures goodness. This bar shows how good Jenny is. This chart shows how good her brother Rick is. If they were perfect the bars would go up to the top of the chart. They have done some good and some bad so the bars are this far up the chart.

One day Jenny went into Rick's room and played with his toys. She tried to change a battery and broke the toy. She did something wrong. So the bar on her goodness chart goes down. *(Tear off some of the first bar.)*

Rick was angry when he saw what she did. He wanted to get even. So he went into Jenny's room and broke one of her toys. Now Rick has done something wrong; so his goodness line goes down. *(Shorten the second bar.)* Now they are even.

When Jenny saw her broken toy she was angry and called Rick bad names. That made her goodness go down again. *(Do it.)* Rick called her bad names to get even and his went down too. *(Do it.)* Then Rick told their mother that Jenny broke the toy on purpose. That was a lie; so his line goes down again. *(Do it.)* Jenny wanted to get even with Rick for lying; so she said she did not break the toy. That was a lie; so her goodness went down. *(Do it.)*

Do you see what happened? When you get even with someone you put yourself down not up. If you get angry because someone did something wrong and decide to get even, you will also do something wrong. Getting even with something that is bad always means doing something bad. Instead of getting even with bad things, you should try to do good things.

Our Bible reading tells of two occasions when we should not try to get even with people who hurt us. The first is that when you get even with another person you sin against that person. If others have sinned against you, they have a problem. Don't add to your problems by sinning against them.

The second is more important. It says you should not get even with others because you love them. You might think it is hard to love people who have hurt you. But remember what Jesus did. He loves us even when we are sinners. Even though we have hurt Jesus he loves us and forgives us. Because he died for us, he gave us his goodness. He came to be on our chart with us. Instead of shoving us down, he gives us his goodness and pulls us up. When Jesus is with you, your chart looks like this: *(Make the bars go to the top.)* If we want to get even with someone, let's get even with Jesus. He loves us. We get even by loving him and others.

# God Will Never Forget You

**THE WORD:**

> God said, "Jerusalem, I can never forget you! I have
> written your name on the palms of my hands."
> > Isaiah 49:16 (Eighth Sunday after the Epiphany)

**THE WORLD:**

> A name tag, the kind that sticks, for each child or for a
> representative group. Pencils. An equal number of tags
> with Jesus' name.

Does anyone ever forget your name? Sometimes uncles,
aunts and parents' friends get kids' names mixed up.
Teachers sometimes have trouble keeping all the names
straight too. Has your teacher ever called you by someone
else's name, or used your name to call another student?
In families with lots of kids, even the parents will sometimes use the wrong name.

We don't like for people to forget our names. But I
can think of something worse. What if God forgot your
name? It's a scary thought that God might get us mixed
up with someone else or forget who we are. But don't
worry about it. In our Bible reading God says, "Jerusalem,
I can never forget you! I have written your name on the
palms of my hands."

God tells the people of Jerusalem he will never forget
them. He mentions Jerusalem because he had a special
relationship with the Jewish people. They were the people God chose to teach his will to the world. God says he
could not forget the people to whom he had given such
a special task.

God also has a reason never to forget your name. His

Son came to die for the sins of the whole world. He rose from the dead to claim all who believe in him as his own people. In Jesus Christ God has put his name on us. We are called Christians. But he also puts our name on himself. He can say to us, "Christians, I can never forget you! I have written your name on the palms of my hands."

I have a name tag for each of you. Put your name on it. *(For a large group have several adults help.)* Now let's imagine that God has our names. Notice what he does with them. He does not put our names on his chest or on his forehead. He couldn't see the names there. Instead he puts the names on the palms of his hands. He sees the names all the time. He never forgets that we are his people because his Son saved us.

God will never forget you. But some people have forgotten God. I don't want you to forget God; so I have a name tag for you with his Son's name on it. *(Give each child a name tag with Jesus' name.)* Don't put the name on your chest or forehead. Put his name on your palm where you can see it. Keep the name tag there for a while and notice how often you will look at your hand and be reminded of Jesus. Then remember how often God looks at his hand and is reminded of you.

Later the tag will come off your hand, but remember Jesus is a part of you. When you were baptized, you received his name. You became a Christian. Remember him and all that he does for you. And remember that God always remembers you.

# Two Gifts on the Mountain

**THE WORD:**

The Lord said to Moses, "Come up the mountain to me, and while you are here, I will give you two stone tablets which contain all the laws that I have written for the instruction of the people."

Exodus 24:12 (Last Sunday after the Epiphany)

**THE WORLD:**

A cross, the Ten Commandments on two posters.

Our Bible reading tells us that God invited Moses to climb to the top of a mountain. God had a special gift for Moses and he wanted to give it to him on a high mountain. Mountain climbing is not easy. Moses was an old man— over 80 years old.

But Moses wanted that gift; so he climbed all the way up that mountain. When he got there God gave him the Ten Commandments written on two stone tablets. Each commandment told Moses he was a sinner. Each commandment told Moses he would have to change his life. What a present! Imagine climbing all the way up that mountain just to be told you are a sinner.

God also has a present for you—the same Ten Commandments. You don't have to climb a mountain to get them. But you have to study. You have to go to classes. Some kids might think it would be easier to climb a mountain than to go to classes. You do all that studying only to learn you are a sinner. Why go to all that work to find out something you'd rather not know?

But that's not all of the story. God invited Moses back up to the top of another mountain. He had another present for Moses. You can read about it in the New Testament, Matthew 17. The story tells us that Jesus went up a mountain with three of his disciples. On that mountain the disciples saw Jesus talking to Moses and Elijah. But Jesus was different. They saw him as Moses saw him and as we will see him in heaven. Jesus showed his victory over sin and death. He showed what life will be like when we are free from all the wrong we have done.

The Ten Commandments were the first gift from a mountain. This cross reminds us of the second gift from the mountain. It tells us that Jesus died to pay for our sins. It says he obeyed the Ten Commandments for us. He prepares a place for us in heaven.

You also climb a mountain for the second gift. You go to classes to learn about the life of Jesus. You learn about him to receive the gift he has for you. This gift brings love, peace, and joy. It helps you live with the problems you have now and tells you that you will be free from those problems in heaven.

Remember, you need both gifts from the mountain. You need to know the Ten Commandments so you know that you need the second gift. God gives us the commandments because he loves us. He wants us to repent and come to him for the greatest of all gifts—Jesus Christ our Savior.

# Who Is Telling the Truth?

**THE WORD:**

The snake replied, "That's not true; you will not die. God said that because he knows that when you eat it, you will be like God and know what is good and what is bad."

Genesis 3:4-5 (First Sunday in Lent)

**THE WORLD:**

A cigarette ad showing someone enjoying a cigarette and the warning that smoking is dangerous to health.

Look at this ad. See the person enjoying the cigarette. This is a happy picture. It makes you think that smoking a cigarette is fun. But look what it says here: "Warning: The Surgeon General has determined that cigarette smoking is dangerous to your health."

Making yourself sick is not fun. People are not happy because they have health problems. Something is wrong with this ad. One part says smoking cigarettes is good. The other says it is dangerous to your health. Who is telling the truth?

This ad is only one example of many in your life when you will have to ask, "Who is telling the truth?" The problem started in the Garden of Eden after God had created Adam and Eve. God told them not to eat from one tree in the garden. He said if they ate from it they would die. They had plenty to eat. They didn't need the fruit from that tree.

But the devil came to them and said, "That's not true; you will not die." God had said, "Don't eat it or you will die." The devil said, "Eat it, you won't die." Which was telling the truth? Adam and Eve believed the devil. They ate the fruit. If the devil had told the truth, Adam and Eve would still be alive today. But he lied. They are dead.

44

God tells us to love him with all our hearts, souls, and minds. But the world tells us to have a good time, take care of ourselves first, think only about what we want to do. Which is telling the truth?

God tells us to worship him, to pray to him, to listen to his word. But people say, "You don't have to go to church. You don't have to read the Bible. You don't have to pray." Which is telling the truth?

God tells us to love other people as we love ourselves. But we often love only ourselves. We think we can call other people bad names. We think we don't have to help others. Who is telling the truth?

We know that God is the One who tells the truth. But God has done more than tell the truth. He sent his Son to be the way, the truth and the life for us. Adam and Eve had to die because they disobeyed God. But God promised them a Savior who would take away the permanent punishment of death and give them life again.

God has also done more than tell you what to do. He sent Jesus to live the perfect life for you. Jesus loves you so much he died for you. He took your punishment. Now we listen to him because we know he speaks the truth to us.

You have to make many choices every day. Many voices will tell you they are speaking the truth and that all other voices are lying. But listen for the voice of God. Hear it in Jesus Christ.

# God Is with You on Every Step

**THE WORD:**

The Lord said to Abram, "Leave your native land, your relatives, and your father's home, and go to a country that I am going to show you. I will give you many descendants, and they will become a great nation. I will bless you and make your name famous, so that you will be a blessing. I will bless those who bless you, but I will curse those who curse you. And through you I will bless all the nations."

Genesis 12:1-3 (Second Sunday in Lent)

**THE WORLD:**

Large blank poster, 5 pieces of color paper 2 inches wide, lengths: 2, 4, 6, 8, 10 inches. A paper-doll figure 3 inches tall. Tape.

---

This *(doll)* is Abram. Later God changed his name to Abraham. God promised him that all the nations of the earth would be blessed through him. Abram must have felt that the promise was impossible for God to keep. When he heard the promise, he must have felt like he was standing next to a 20-foot pole and was told to jump to the top. *(Put the doll on the poster next to the 10" paper.)*

But God gave other promises to Abram too. *(As each promise is mentioned add a paper to form steps going down.)* He promised Abram that he would become famous. *(Add 8".)* Abram couldn't imagine himself being famous. God said Abram would be the start of a great nation *(add 6")*. That must have been too much for Abram to accept. God told Abram he would be the father of many descendants even though he was 75 years old and had no children. *(Add 4".)*

God also told Abram to leave his family and go to a new

land. *(Place 2" piece next to the 4".)* With God's help Abram could see himself doing that. God helped Abram move to the new land. *(Place the doll on the first step and continue to advance it with each promise fulfilled.)* God did give Abram a son, who had two sons, who had many sons. God did make the descendants of one of those grandsons into a great nation. And from that great nation came Jesus, who is the Savior of the world. In him all the nations of the earth have been blessed. God kept all his promises to Abram. God was with him on every step. *(Remove all the steps.)*

Now this doll is you. God has also given you many promises. He has promised you will live forever with him in heaven. *(Put up 10" paper.)* It's too far for us to jump from here to heaven. God also promises to be with you now. *(Add 8".)* Imagine—God with you all the time. He promises to forgive all your sins. *(Add 6".)* He promises to love you. *(Add 4".)* He came to live with you and to die for your sins. *(Add 2".)*

That first step makes it possible for us to receive the promises of God. All of his promises are like steps. Each step is too tall for us to make by ourselves. But God helps us up each step. First he sent Jesus to come to be with us, to live with us, to suffer for us. *(Place figure on the first step and advance as each promise is fulfilled.)* Then we can see his love for us—and his forgiveness. Then we can know he is with us now. And we will be with him in heaven forever.

God is with you on every step.

# Be Led by God's Eyes

**THE WORD:**

God says, "I will lead my blind people by roads they have never traveled. I will turn their darkness into light and make rough country smooth before them. These are my promises, and I will keep them without fail."

Isaiah 42:16 (Third Sunday in Lent)

**THE WORLD:**

A blindfold for a child and a guide. (Communion rail used here. If not available, tie a rope between two stationary objects.)

To understand the Bible reading for today, you need to understand what it is like to be blind. Jeff, will you put on this blindfold? Now Jeff can't see. He can't walk around the room without bumping into things.

Come here, Jeff, and feel this rail. See how you can use the rail as a guide. You can walk when you keep one hand on the rail and follow it. *(Help the child walk back and forth along the rail.)* Now Jeff can walk even though he cannot see. But he can only walk on one path. He can go only where the rail goes.

But Jeff could have another kind of guide. Here—take my hand. I will be your guide. Now you can walk over here. You can go around the pulpit. You can go many places when I am your guide.

God tells us that our sin makes us spiritually blind. We can still see the world—but we can't see God. Our sin blinds us so we cannot live the way God planned for us to live. Because we are blind in sin, we have only one way to live—the life of a sinner. We keep going the same way, doing the same wrong. We are like Jeff who had to walk back and forth on the same path when the rail was his only guide.

But listen to what God says in our Bible reading, "I will lead my blind people by roads they have never traveled. I will turn their darkness into light and make rough country smooth before them. These are my promises and I will keep them without fail."

God knows we are blind and can't see him. But he can still see us. And he says we are still his people. He does not want us to follow the path of sin. So he promises to send his Son to lead us on another road. He promises that his Son would give us light instead of darkness; that he would make the rough road smooth.

God kept his promises when Jesus came to earth. Even though he was always good and holy, Jesus traveled on that path of sin. The path led him to the cross and death. But by his death he paid the price of sin. He came back to life to be with us and to lead us back to God.

Even though we are still sinners and by ourselves still follow the path of sin, we can now walk in new ways. Jesus is with us. He is the guide who takes us by the hand and leads us to God. He gives us the way to love and serve God. He gives us the way to love and serve one another. He leads us through life here on earth. He will also lead us to heaven.

# When Will You Ask for Help?

**THE WORD:**

God said, "I will abandon my people until they have suffered enough for their sins and come looking for me. Perhaps in their suffering they will try to find me."

Hosea 5:15 (Fourth Sunday in Lent)

**THE WORLD:**

Bottle of medicine that does not taste good—Kaopectate used here as an example.

Eric woke up one morning with a stomachache. His mother said, "There's a lot of stomach flu going around. You'd better take some of this (the Kaopectate).

But Eric had taken this medicine before. He knew it didn't taste good. He said, "It doesn't hurt much. I'll be okay."

Then his stomach hurt even more. He had to go to the bathroom several times. His mother said, "You'd better take some of the medicine." But Eric remembered the taste and refused.

Instead of going away, Eric's pain got worse. Finally the pain made him forget how bad the medicine tasted. Instead he thought about how much he hurt. So he asked his mother, "May I have some of the medicine?" He took two spoonfuls and the pain started to go away. He still felt sick, but he knew he was getting better. After several more doses Eric was well again.

Think about that story as you listen to the Bible reading for today. God says, "I will abandon my people until they have suffered enough for their sins and come looking for me. Perhaps in their suffering they will try to find me."

God tells us we are often like Eric in the story. We know we have sinned. We feel bad because we have done wrong things. God is like the mother in the story. He offers to help us. He wants to forgive us. Jesus had to suffer and die for us. We don't like to hear about our sin and his suffering. We don't like to repent and ask for forgiveness. All of that is like bad-tasting medicine. So we say, "No, God, I'll take care of myself."

God says he has to let us go. He won't force us to repent and come to him for forgiveness. But when we refuse his help the pain of our sin gets greater and greater. We become more unhappy with ourselves. We get more people mad at us because of the way we behave. Finally our pain is so bad we have to go back to God for help. We say, "Lord, will you forgive me?"

And God says, "Yes." He is always ready to forgive us. He is always ready to help us in our fight against sin. The question is: When will you ask him for help? Will you wait until the pain is so great that you can't stand it? Will you wait until you have hurt yourself and others? He wants to forgive you every day. He wants to keep you close to him so he can share in the pain of your sin and you can share in the love that Jesus gives to you.

# New Life from Dry Bones

**THE WORD:**

> (God) said to me, "Mortal man, can these bones come back to life?" I replied, "Sovereign Lord, only you can answer that!" God said to me, "Mortal man, the people of Israel are like these bones. They say that they are dried up, without any hope and with no future. . . . I will put my breath in them, bring them back to life, and let them live in their own land. Then they will know I am the Lord."
>
> Ezekiel 37:3, 11, 14a (Fifth Sunday in Lent)

**THE WORLD:**

Package of instant soup, thermos of hot water, cup.

---

If you were hungry, you might like a cup of soup. Here's some soup. *(Offer the dried contents of the package.)* That wouldn't taste so good, would it? But if I put the dried soup in a cup, added hot water and stirred it *(do it)*, I have a nice cup of hot soup. Without the hot water, you would not have eaten the soup. Now it is delicious.

God once showed the prophet Ezekiel a valley filled with dry bones. They were the skeletons of people who had died. There was no life in the valley of the dry bones. God said that the living people were like the skeletons. They had no life. They had no hope and no future. They were like the dry soup—worth nothing the way they were.

God told Ezekiel to speak to the dry bones and tell them that God would put life back into them. The Spirit of God made the bones come back to life. The skeletons had flesh again. The bodies became alive. When the hot water was added to the dried contents of this package, it became soup. When the power of God's Spirit came to the bones in the valley, the people came back to life.

The great miracle is not just that God could raise those dead bones to life. The miracle is also that God can bring life back to us. Sometimes we are like the people of Israel were at that time. We have no hope—no future. Sometimes we feel all dried up, with no joy or purpose in our lives. Though our bodies are still alive, our spirits die. We are like the dried soup, or the valley of dry bones.

But the hot water made the dry soup delicious. The Spirit of God gave life to the skeletons. And Jesus Christ gives us a new life. We can have hope and joy. We can have a future. We can have a good life on this earth—and a life that lasts forever in heaven.

God offers us that new life in Jesus Christ. Because Jesus is our Savior he shared our pain and sorrow of sin. When he suffered and died he became a part of the valley of the dry bones. But he was raised from the dead and by his power we also have a new life.

You will use instant foods often. You will have instant coffee and other things that are tasteless unless you add water. Each time you use instant food, remember the valley of the dry bones. Remember the water of your baptism and know that God has given you a new life in Jesus Christ.

# What Does God
# Have to Say Today?

**THE WORD:**

The Sovereign Lord has taught me what to say, so that I can strengthen the weary. Every morning he makes me eager to hear what he is going to teach me.

Isaiah 50:4 (The Sunday of the Passion—Palm Sunday)

**THE WORLD:**

A cassette recorder.

I am going to teach you something today. To make sure I teach you the right lesson I will record it on this cassette. Listen carefully to what I teach you. *(Record as you read.)* "The Sovereign Lord has taught me what to say, so that I can strengthen the weary. Every morning he makes me eager to hear what he is going to teach me."

Did you learn the lesson? Can you say it back to me? The record player can repeat it word for word. Listen: *(Play the tape.)* Does that mean the record player learned the lesson better than you? No. You have learned more than the machine. Let me tell you why.

The words I want to teach you tell you that God teaches what to say so we can help the weary. The weary people are those who are worried and afraid. Those who feel like giving up are weary. They need to be told that Jesus loves them. But they don't just need recorded words repeated to them. They need Jesus' love applied to their lives.

Sometimes the weary people need to hear that Jesus suffered and died for them; so they will know they are not alone in their suffering. Sometimes they need to hear how Jesus rose from the dead; so they don't have to be afraid to die. Sometimes they need to know that Jesus is with them at all times; so they know God is always there to help.

God has given us many things to say to those who are weary—just as he has many things to say to us when we are weary. That's why our Bible reading says, "Every morning he makes me eager to hear what he is going to teach me." God has something to say to you every day. You can be excited about each day as you wonder how God will share the day with you. He is always with you. He always has something to say to you. He always wants to listen to you.

God's message to you is not words on a recorder that are repeated over and over again in the same way. His message is new every day. His message of forgiveness in Jesus Christ is new today because it tells you that today's sins are forgiven. The story of Christ's suffering is new every day as you see his suffering as a part of your life. His resurrection from the dead is news each day; because he is still alive and still with you.

The tape recorder is able to repeat the words of our Bible reading better than any of you. But you have more than the words. You have the faith that tells you that God is with you. You have a message of comfort and help for the weary. You know that God has something to say to you today. And he'll have something new to say to you tomorrow too.

# A Savior to Be Seen

**THE WORD:**

But God raised him (Jesus) from death three days later and caused him to appear, not to everyone, but only to the witnesses that God had already chosen, that is, to us who ate and drank with him after he rose from death.

Acts 10:40-41 (Easter Sunday)

**THE WORLD:**

Six pictures drawn by children and a first place ribbon.

---

A school sponsored an art contest and each student drew a picture. The judge chose these pictures to be on the bulletin board. Then the judge picked this picture as the best. It wins the first prize *(attach ribbon)*.

A reporter took a picture of the student who drew the picture and the newspaper had a story about the art contest. When people visited the school they wanted to see the picture that won first prize. Do you think the school put the picture in a closet? Of course not, the picture, with the ribbon, would be in the hallway where everyone could see it.

Now let's think of death as being like the art show. All people die just as all the children drew a picture. Some people's death gets more attention than others. When a famous person dies we hear about it in the news. That is like the best pictures being put on the bulletin board.

But the one death that wins first prize is the death of Jesus Christ. Listen to what our Bible reading says about him, "But God raised him from death three days later." Other people's deaths get attention because of what they did *before* they died. Jesus' death gets first prize because of what he did both *before* and *after* he died.

The resurrection of Jesus from the dead has become the

biggest news item in all history. Today people in all parts of the world celebrate because Jesus is alive. Each Sunday we come together as believers in Christ to worship him because he is alive.

Remember, the school didn't hide the picture that won first prize. We can't hide a living Savior either. People want to see the One who won first prize in death by coming back to life again. The Bible reading says, "(God) caused him to appear, not to everyone, but only to the witnesses that God has already chosen, that is, to us who ate and drank with him after he rose from death."

God wants us to see the risen Savior. Peter, who spoke the words of our Bible reading, saw Jesus after his resurrection. Peter ate and drank with Jesus.

God has also chosen us to see Jesus today. We can't see him in the way Peter did. To have Jesus here to eat and to drink with us would limit him to one place. Instead, Jesus is alive with all people everywhere.

We can see the living Jesus by what he does for us. He forgives us when we are wrong and helps us forgive others. He loves us and helps us love others. He tells us that when we die he will share his first place ribbon for a successful death with us. He will raise us from the dead too.

# Don't Quit Halfway Through

**THE WORD:**

Peter said, "In accordance with his own plan God had already decided that Jesus would be handed over to you; and you killed him by letting sinful men crucify him. But God raised him from death, setting him free from its power, because it was impossible that death should hold him prisoner.

Acts 2:23-24 (Second Sunday of Easter)

**THE WORLD:**

Cut flowers in a vase with water, extra water, empty container, scissors, sheet of instructions (as used below).

Cut flowers like these are pretty. But they often wilt in a few days. Here is a plan to make cut flowers last longer. Let's follow the plan and see if it works.

The first step is to remove the flowers from the vase and throw away the stale water. *(Do it.)* Next it tells us to cut off the stems so the fresh cut will allow the flowers to drink more water. *(Do it.)* There. I have followed the instructions. *(Put the flowers back in the vase without water.)*

Do you think the flowers will last longer now? Of course not. They will wilt because they have no water. You can see what happened. I didn't follow the plan all the way. The last instruction says: "Put fresh water in the vase and rearrange the flowers." *(Do it.)* Now I have completed the plan. The flowers have a fresh start.

That's a plan for making flowers last longer. Now let me read you God's plan for saving people forever. "In accordance with his own plan God had already decided that Jesus would be handed over to you." That's step one. God planned for Jesus to be betrayed to people who hated him. Now let's read step two: "And you killed him by letting sinful men crucify him." That's step two. God let Christ be killed on the cross.

We sometimes wonder how God could plan such things. A plan to let his son be betrayed and killed on a cross is not good. That's a bad plan. But God didn't stop the plan halfway through. Listen to the next step. "But God raised him from death, setting him free from its power, because it was impossible that death should hold him prisoner." God could plan Christ's betrayal and death, because he also planned his resurrection from the dead. God didn't stop halfway through the plan. He completed his plan to save us when Christ rose from the dead.

Remember God's complete plan. Don't stop halfway through. God started his plan in you when you were baptized. He has helped you grow in faith. If you have trouble or difficulties, don't think that God has failed you. Remember his plan. The plan is not complete until you are in heaven with him. He will stay with you and help you through the parts of life that are difficult, just as he was with Jesus during that suffering and death.

Don't stop halfway through. Stay with the plan that God has made for you.

# Look at God's Menu

**THE WORD:**

Peter said to them, "Each one of you must turn away from his sins and be baptized in the name of Jesus Christ, so that your sins will be forgiven; and you will receive God's gift, the Holy Spirit. For God's promise was made to you and your children, and to all who are far away—all whom the Lord our God calls to himself."

Acts 2:38-39 (Third Sunday of Easter)

**THE WORLD:**

A menu from a restaurant—borrow or make one.

Do you like to eat in a restaurant? I think it is fun to look over the menu and decide what I want. On this menu I will take the chicken dinner. The waitress says that with the chicken I also get a salad and french fries. Isn't that nice! I order chicken, but I also get extras.

Of course, sometimes you can't get what is on the menu. You have to check the price to see if you can pay for it. Sometimes the menu will say, "On Friday Only"; so I couldn't order that on Sunday. Or the waitress might say, "Sorry, we're out of chicken today."

Think of the Bible as God's menu. In it he lists the blessings he wants you to have. In Genesis 2 *(show it)* he tells how he created us. The menu offers us God who is our Father. In Exodus 20 we read his Law. The menu says God loves us enough to care what we do. He doesn't want us to hurt ourselves or others. In Matthew 6, he tells us he will give us the food and clothing we need. In Matthew 27 he tells us he died for our sins. The next chapter tells us he came back from the dead; so we can have eternal life with him.

Isn't it fun to look at the Bible as a menu to see all the things that God offers to us? The Bible reading for today offers one of God's specials. Peter says, "Each one of you must turn away from your sins and be baptized in the name of Jesus Christ." Baptism is one of many gifts that God wants you to have. He offers to wash you clean in the name of Jesus your Savior.

Remember when I ordered chicken and got the salad and french fries too? Other things also come with baptism. When you are baptized, Peter tells you that you also receive the forgiveness of sins and God's gift, the Holy Spirit. Baptism always includes forgiveness because you are baptized in the name of Jesus who forgives sins. Baptism always gives the gift of the Holy Spirit because you are also baptized in his name.

When you want baptism from God's menu, you don't have to worry about paying for it, or if it's the right day, or if it is still available. Peter says, "God's promise was made to you and your children and to all who are far away —all whom the Lord our God calls to himself." God offers baptism to everyone. It is already paid for. He wants all people to have the forgiveness of sins and the gift of the Holy Spirit.

If you are not baptized, then look at God's menu and receive what he offers you. If you have been baptized, remember you still have it. Because you are baptized in the name of Christ, you live in Christ. Each day he gives you forgiveness of sins. Each day, his Holy Spirit is with you.

# When God Talks, Listen!

**THE WORD:**

"How stubborn you are!" Stephen went on to say. "How heathen your hearts, how deaf you are to God's message! You are just like your ancestors: you too have always resisted the Holy Spirit!"

Acts 7:51 (Fourth Sunday of Easter)

**THE WORLD:**

A note in an envelope—see message below.

Kevin came home from school and went to the refrigerator to get something to eat. He saw this note stuck on the door of the refrigerator. It had his name on it. He knew the note was from his mother. He also knew what it would say. His mother would tell him to clean his room.

Kevin didn't want to clean his room. He wanted to go out to the park where the kids were having a skateboard contest. But his skateboard was broken. Since he couldn't enter the contest he did not want to watch someone else win. And he didn't want to clean his room either. So Kevin watched a rerun of an old TV show that he didn't even like.

When his mother came home she was surprised to see Kevin. She asked if he had read the note. He said he hadn't seen it. "You'd better read it now," she said. The note said, "Dear Kevin: Please clean your room. When you have finished look under the bed. I have a surprise for you. Love, Mom." Kevin rushed to look under his bed. He found a new skateboard. But it was too late. The contest was over.

In our Bible reading Stephen said that the people of his day were like Kevin. God had given them a message.

But they didn't want to hear it. They knew what the message was. God would tell them they were sinners. He would say that they have to change the way they live. But they did not want to change; so they wouldn't listen to the message.

Would Stephen say the same thing to you? Are you too stubborn to hear God's message. Do you think you already know everything God has to say; so you don't have to listen any more? Many people don't read the Bible or go to church because they think they know what God has to say to them. They don't want to be told about their sins. They don't want their lives to be changed.

If you listen to God's word, he will tell you about your sin, but he will also tell you about the Savior who died to pay for your sin. If you listen to God's word, he will tell you to change your life, but he will also tell you that Jesus rose from the dead to give you a new life.

When God talks, listen. Don't be afraid to hear what he has to say. He loves you. He shows that love in what he has done for you.

# A Way to Be Open-Minded

**THE WORD:**

The people there (Berea) were more open-minded than the people in Thessalonica. They listened to the message with great eagerness, and every day they studied the Scriptures to see if what Paul said was really true.

Acts 17:11 (Fifth Sunday of Easter)

**THE WORLD:**

A set of small blocks plus an assortment of larger blocks, a box with a lid and an extra lid with a hole the size of the small blocks.

Paul and Silas were missionaries who went to Thessalonica to tell the people about Jesus. But the people in Thessalonica were closed-minded. They would not listen to the story about Jesus. They did not want to hear about their sins and the Savior from their sins.

Those people were like this box. See—it is closed. I would like to put these blocks into the box, but I can't get them in as long as the box is closed. Do you think you have a closed mind? Will you listen to what God tells you? Do you think you already know all the answers so you don't need to learn more? Are you afraid of new ideas? Check yourself to see if your mind is closed so new ideas can't get in.

Then Paul and Silas went to Berea. The Bereans were open-minded. They listened to what Paul and Silas had to say. They were like a box without a lid.

If closed-mindedness is bad because it keeps us from learning, it seems that being open-minded would always be good. But being open-minded can also cause problems. I wanted to put this set of blocks into the box. When the lid is off the blocks can go in—but a lot of other things can go in also. An open-minded person receives many new ideas, but not all of them are good. If the Bereans were so open-minded that they believed everything they heard, they would have believed in many false gods also.

However the Bereans were open-minded in a good way. When they heard Paul and Silas preach, they checked what they heard with the Bible. They discovered that the Old Testament told about a Messiah who would die to pay for their sins and who would become the victorious Lord of all. So they believed what Paul and Silas said.

The Bereans were open-minded like this. See the box has a lid, but it has a hole that lets the blocks that belong inside go through. These larger blocks that don't belong in the box cannot go through.

We also can be open-minded this way. We have to listen to new ideas and new ways of thinking. We don't have to be afraid to listen to others. But we also have to check those ideas out by listening to what God's word says. Then we can sort out the things that agree with God's message to us from those that are against God's word.

Remember the Bereans as good examples of open-minded people who checked the Scripture. Because they listened to Paul and Silas they learned that Jesus was their Savior. I offer you that same message today. Check the Scripture and you will find that it is true. Jesus is your Savior.

# Find What You Already Have

**THE WORD:**

Paul said, "For as I walked through your city and looked at the places where you worship, I found an altar on which is written, 'To an Unknown God.' That which you worship, then, even though you do not know it, is what I now proclaim to you."

Acts 17:23 (Sixth Sunday of Easter)

**THE WORLD:**

A Bible with a ten dollar bill at Acts 17.

When Becky left for a month at summer camp her mother gave her this Bible and told her to read it every day. Her mother suggested that Becky read the book of Acts. Becky said she would and packed the Bible in her suitcase.

At camp Becky was busy so she forgot to read the Bible. She liked the camp but she had one problem. She ran out of money to buy treats after the campfire each evening. She phoned her mother and asked for money but her mother said, "You already have enough money."

During the last week of camp Becky found her Bible and remembered she had promised to read it. She started reading Acts — and look what she found *(show the money)*. She had had the money all the time, but she didn't know it was there.

When Becky read the Bible she found the story that is our lesson for today. Paul went to Athens, a city in Greece, and found that the people were religious. They wanted to worship God, but they didn't know who he was. They even had an altar that said, "To an Unknown God." They were like Becky. She had money but didn't know it. They had a God, but didn't know who he was.

Paul said to the people, "That which you worship, then, even though you do not know it, is what I now proclaim to you." Just as Becky found the money she already had, Paul came to tell the people about the God they already had. Paul wanted the people of Athens to know who God was. He told them that God had created them. He told them God cared about them and wanted them to turn away from their sin. He also told them God had sent his Son Jesus to be their Savior to come back from the dead to give eternal life.

You have something more important than ten dollars in the pages of your Bible. The Bible tells you God's message for you. If you know there is a God, but do not know that he loves you and is with you, you have an unknown God. But God knows you and loves you. He wants you to know him and love him. He sent his Son to be your Savior so you could know him. You can love him because he already loves you.

Remember the story of Becky and the money in her Bible. Then remember what you have in your Bible. It tells you the way of salvation through Jesus Christ. It shows that God knows you—and you can know him.

# God's Delivery System

**THE WORD:**

Jesus said, "But when the Holy Spirit comes upon you, you will be filled with power, and you will be witnesses for me in Jerusalem, in all of Judea and Samaria, and to the ends of the earth."

Acts 1:8 (Seventh Sunday of Easter)

**THE WORLD:**

Three envelopes addressed to friends in the area, several states away, and a foreign country. Postage stamps.

---

I have three messages that I want delivered. *(Show the envelopes.)* This one is to _____ who lives about _____ miles away. This letter is to _____ who lives in _____. That's about _____ miles from here. Look at this one. It's to _____ who lives in _____. That's so far away that I don't know how many miles it is.

How do you think I can get these messages delivered to my friends? Let's try the one that is the nearest first. Can I throw this envelope that far? No, I can't throw it more than a few feet. I could carry this one to the address in town. But this one is to someone several states away. And this one is to go half way around the world. How can I get these messages to my friends?

You know the way, don't you? I add a stamp to each envelope. Once I have put this stamp on each envelope, the one to a foreign country takes more stamps, I can drop the letters in a post office box and they will be delivered. Without stamps the letters wouldn't go anywhere. With the stamps they will be delivered to the people whose addresses are on the envelopes.

Right before Jesus went to be on the right hand of his Father in heaven, he told the disciples to deliver a message for him. The message was that Jesus is the Savior of the world. They were to tell people that Jesus had come from God to be a person on earth, that he had died for everyone's sin, that he came back from the dead to give all people a new life. Jesus said they were to deliver the message to people in Jerusalem (that's like the letter to someone here in town) to all of Judea and Samaria (that's like the letter to someone in another state) and to the ends of the earth (that's like my letter to a friend half way around the world).

The disciples knew the message they were to deliver. They knew who was to receive the message. But they needed a way to get the message from themselves to others. They needed something like the stamps I put on these messages. But Jesus also gave them the way to deliver the message. He told them about God's delivery system. He said, "But when the Holy Spirit comes upon you, you will be filled with power."

The Holy Spirit is God's delivery system. He helps those who believe in Jesus to send the message of Christ to other people. The stamps on these letters make the letters go to whomever they are addressed. So also the Holy Spirit's power carries the message of Jesus from us to other people.

You know that Jesus is your Savior. The message has come to you because the Holy Spirit has sent others to tell you about Jesus. Now the Holy Spirit works through you to give you the power to send the message to others.

# God Pours His Spirit on You

**THE WORD:**

God said, "Afterward I will pour out my spirit on everyone: your sons and daughters will proclaim my message; your old men will have dreams, and your young men will see visions. At that time I will pour out my spirit even on servants, both men and women."

Joel 2:28-29 (The Day of Pentecost)

**THE WORLD:**

A dry sponge, a flat dish, a pitcher of water.

In our Bible reading for today God promises to pour out his Spirit on everyone. He kept that promise on the first Christian Pentecost when the Holy Spirit came to the people who spoke and the people who listened to the word of God.

God still keeps that promise today. He pours his Spirit on us when we hear the message that Jesus Christ is our Savior. When Peter preached about the death and resurrection of Christ, the Bible says, "The Holy Spirit came down on all those who were listening to his message" (Acts 10:44).

Let's see what happens to us when God pours his Holy Spirit on us. Before the Spirit is poured on us we are like this sponge. The sponge is dry and hard. Many people keep sponges to wipe off the refrigerator or stove. But this sponge would not wipe off anything. It might even scratch the surface instead of cleaning off the mess.

Without the Holy Spirit we are like the dry sponge because we cannot do the things we are supposed to do. Just as the sponge has a purpose, we have all been created for a purpose. God made us to serve him and to love other people. But by ourselves we can do neither.

Then God pours his Spirit on us. (Put the sponge in the flat dish and pour water on it.) God pours himself on us when we are baptized in the name of the Father and of the Son and of the Holy Spirit. When the Holy Spirit is poured on us he brings us the message that Jesus Christ is our Savior. In Jesus we see how God loves us and all people—so we can love ourselves and others. God has served us by sending Christ to die for us and to give us a new life. So we can serve him by sharing his love with others both by what we say and what we do.

Now look at the sponge. It looks different. It feels different. It is different. The water in the sponge has made it soft. Now it can wipe up a mess. Now it can do what it was made to do.

You are different because God has poured his Holy Spirit on you. As water was added to the sponge, God has added the love of Jesus to your life. Because he has given you that love, you can give the love to others.

But you know what would happen to the sponge if it were left alone. It would become dry and hard again. More water must be poured on it to keep it moist and soft. The Holy Spirit also continues to pour the love of Jesus on you. You need to receive that love every day; so you can give it every day.

# Search the Past

**THE WORD:**

Search the past, the time before you were born, all the way back to the time when God created man on the earth. Search the entire earth. Has anything as great as this ever happened before? Has anyone ever heard of anything like this?

Deuteronomy 4:32 (First Sunday after Pentecost)

**THE WORLD:**

A box labeled "The Past" containing a baptism certificate, a Bible, a cross, and a rock.

See what this box is—the past. The past is everything that has already happened. What you did yesterday is part of the past. What happened a thousand years ago is part of the past.

Our Bible reading says, "Search the past, the time before you were born, all the way back to the time when God created man on the earth." Of course, the past can't be put in a box like this, but we'll pretend this is the past so we can search through it.

First we'll search through your past. You aren't old enough to have a long past. But look what I found (certificate). All of you have been baptized in the past. This goes back to the time you were born and then born again in your baptism. In your baptism you were washed clean in the name of the Father and of the Son and of the Holy Spirit.

But God tells us to search the past before we were born. Way back in the past we find this (the Bible). This Bible was printed only a few years ago but some of it was written more than 2000 years ago. Now we are searching far in the past.

As we search we find this (the cross). The cross reminds us of the most important thing that ever happened. God's Son, Jesus Christ, died for our sins. He rose from the dead to give us eternal life.

We can search even farther into the past. Here is a rock —a part of the world that God created in the beginning— as far back as the past can go.

God tells us to search the past so that we can see the great things he has done. When we search back to the beginning of time, we find God at work. We see how he created the world and how he created us. We know he is our Father.

Even though all people sinned, God did not give up his creation. Remember how we searched and found the death and resurrection of Jesus in the past. Then we saw how God's Son is our Savior.

When we read about Jesus' love for us from the Bible, the Holy Spirit gives us faith and makes our faith grow. Through the Word, the Holy Spirit gives us the blessings Jesus has earned for us.

When we search the past we see what God the Father, God the Son, and God the Holy Spirit have done in history.

Now that we've searched the past we can look at the present and the future. Remember your baptism. You were baptized in the name of the Father, Son, and Holy Spirit. All that God has done in the past, he does for you now. Because God has done great things in the past, he will do those great things in your future.

# God Gives You a Choice

**THE WORD:**

Moses said, "Today I am giving you the choice between a blessing and a curse—a blessing, if you obey the commands of the Lord your God that I am giving you today; but a curse, if you disobey these commands and turn away to worship other gods that you have never worshiped before."

Deuteronomy 11:26-28 (Second Sunday after Pentecost)

**THE WORLD:**

A bottle of prescription medicine.

Through Moses God offers you a choice. Do you want a blessing or a curse? A blessing is a good gift from God. Our food, health, and other good things are blessings from God. His greatest blessing is forgiveness and eternal life in heaven.

A curse is a punishment. It is a curse to be separated from God.

If you have a choice between a curse and a blessing, you will take the blessing. Right? Strange as it may seem, some people choose the curse. I do not want you to make that choice. So let's talk about the choice God gives us.

First an example, so we can understand the choice. Suppose you are sick. You had no choice about being sick. But a doctor gives you this medicine which will control your sickness. You still have the disease but as long as you take one of these pills you will not have pain.

Of course you take the medicine. But some people want to stay stick. When they are sick they don't have to go to school. They don't have to work at home. When they are

74

sick everyone feels sorry for them. So they choose to stay sick. That's a bad choice.

Our sin is a sickness. We did not choose to be sinners. We had no choice. But Jesus came to be our Savior. He died to pay for our sins. He is like the medicine. He takes away the pain of our sin. He forgives us each day.

Now we have a choice. Do you want the forgiveness that Jesus gives you? Will you be sorry for your sin and let Christ take your guilt?

Some people would rather keep their sin. They use their sin as an excuse not to serve God. They enjoy their sin and refuse to be sorry. But when they choose sin, they also choose a curse.

God gives you a choice between a curse and a blessing. You have a curse if you break God's law, a blessing if you obey the law. By yourself, you have no choice. But you are not by yourself. Christ is with you. He forgives you when you break the law. He obeys it for you. When you believe in Christ as your Savior, your choice is a blessing.

# Love That Lasts

**THE WORD:**

But the Lord says, "Israel and Judah, what am I going to do with you? Your love for me disappears as quickly as morning mist; it is like dew, that vanishes early in the day. . . . I want your constant love, not your animal sacrifices. I would rather have my people know me than have them burn offerings to me."

Hosea 6:4 and 6 (Third Sunday after Pentecost)

**THE WORLD:**

A mirror, a board, paint, and a paintbrush.

Do you love God? Of course you love God. You love him because he loves you and gave his Son to be your Savior. But how do you love God? Some people just talk about loving God. But love is more than saying, "I love you." Love is a part of the way we live.

A long time ago God had a problem with the people of Israel and Judah. He said, "What am I going to do with you? Your love for me disappears as quickly as morning mist; it is like dew, that vanishes early in the day." Does God have that same problem with us today?

Those people talked about loving God. But it was just talk. They forgot their love as soon as they said it. God said their love was like the mist or the morning dew. It soon disappeared. You can understand what God meant by looking at this mirror. See my breath on the mirror *(breathe on it)*. Look what happens. It disappears in a few seconds.

Is your love for God like my breath on the mirror? Do you love God while you are in church, then forget him when you are at home?

God says, "I want your constant love." He wants love that will last. Your love for God should not be like breath on a mirror. Instead it should be like this *(brush paint on the board)*. The paint does not disappear in a few seconds. Instead it dries and stays on the board. The paint will last. And God wants your love for him to last. He wants you to love him now, and he also wants you to love him tomorrow and the rest of the week. He wants you to love him here in church, and also at home, when you are playing with friends, when you are on vacation. God wants you to love him now and also when you become a teenager, an adult, and a senior citizen.

God has given you a way to make your love for him last. Remember why you love God. You love him because he loves you. He does not give you love that lasts only a short time. His love is not like breath on a mirror. He gave you love that will last forever. His love is given by Jesus Christ who died on the cross to pay for your sins. His love is like the paint on the board. As the paint is put on the board it changes the board's color and becomes a part of the board. Christ changes you and becomes a part of you.

As long as you receive the love that God has given you in Christ, you will have love for God that lasts.

# Watch What Deal You Accept

**THE WORD:**

The Lord said, "Now, if you will obey me and keep my covenant, you will be my own people . . ." Then all of the people answered together, "We will do everything that the Lord has said," and Moses reported this to the Lord.

Exodus 19:5a, 8 (Fourth Sunday after Pentecost)

**THE WORLD:**

A roll of tickets.

---

Let's pretend we are going on a trip and I am the tour leader. If I am the leader, you have to promise that you will do what I tell you to do. Do you all promise? Okay, let's go on the trip.

First, we get on the bus. Here's my ticket *(show one ticket)*. I'll give my ticket to the driver. Now you give your ticket to him.

Remember, you promised to do what I told you to do. And I said give the driver a ticket. I'm sorry if you don't have a ticket. That's your problem. You promised to do what I told you.

We have a problem, don't we? Maybe our problem will help us understand the Bible reading. God said to the people, "Now, if you will obey me and keep my covenant, you will be my own people." God offered to make a deal with the people of Israel like I made with you. God said that he would be their God if they would do what he told them to do. And all the people answered, "We will do everything that the Lord has said."

Do you know what happened? God told them not to worship idols. But the people made a golden calf and worshiped it. God gave them other commandments. And someone broke every one of the laws God gave. They accepted the deal God offered them. God kept his part of the deal. But the people broke theirs. I also kept my part of the deal when I gave the driver a ticket for myself. I asked you to do what I told you to do, but you could not do it. The people of Israel could not do what God asked them to do either.

Would you accept the deal that God offered those people? Better think about it. If you accept that deal you will have to be perfect.

Back to my being your tour leader. Here, I have a ticket for each of you. I give you a ticket. *(Do it.)* Now you can do what I say. You can give a ticket to the driver and we take the tour.

Jesus also has something to give to you. He became a person who lived under the Law of God. Jesus obeyed the law perfectly. He had his ticket to be with God. But he also died for us to give each of us a ticket also. He kept the law for us. He did what we could not do.

We do not live under the deal that we have to obey God in order for us to be his children. We are God's children because Jesus has saved us. We can be with God now and forever, not because we kept the deal, but because Jesus kept the deal for us and we believe in him.

# Think Before You Quit

**THE WORD:**

Jeremiah said, "Lord, you have deceived me, and I was deceived. You are stronger than I am, and you have overpowered me. Everyone makes fun of me; they laugh at me all day long. . . . But when I say, 'I will forget the Lord and no longer speak in his name'; then your message is like a fire burning deep within me. I try my best to hold it in, but can no longer keep it back."

Jeremiah 20:7 and 9 (Fifth Sunday after Pentecost)

**THE WORLD:**

A large picnic basket filled to make it heavy.

It's time for picnics. Let's imagine you and your friends are going to (local recreation area). You're going for the day; so your mother packs this basket for you. It has sandwiches, lemonade, fried chicken, and potato chips.

It is heavy. Bobby, will you carry the basket? You'd move slowly with that and the rest of the kids would rush ahead. They might even laugh and say, "Can't you keep up?" That could upset you. The food is for them too. You could think about leaving the basket. But then you'd have no food for yourself. And none for your friends. When you think about carrying the basket, you want to leave it. When you think about eating and drinking what is in it, you want to take it along.

Remember that story as we talk about the Bible lesson. God told Jeremiah to warn the people to change their ways so he could help them. That was a big job—like carrying the basket. Jeremiah tried to do what God asked, but listen to what he says, "Lord, you have deceived me, and I was deceived. You are stronger than I am, and you have overpowered me. Everyone makes fun of me; they laugh at me all day long."

Jeremiah wanted to quit his job as prophet. He said, "But when I say, 'I will forget the Lord and no longer speak in his name,' then your message is like a fire burning deep within me. I try my best to hold it in, but can no longer keep it back."

When Jeremiah thought about quitting, he remembered the job God gave him. He knew if he did not give God's warning the people would leave God. He didn't like the job, but he wanted the people to be with God. So he didn't quit.

We can be in the same situation. Jesus carried our load of sin to the cross. He died to give us love and forgiveness. We are free from the load of sin, but we do have the love and forgiveness. God has told us to tell other people about Jesus. We are to love and serve our Savior. Sometimes that is a big load. The people we want to help laugh at us. They can do other things while we serve God. We feel like quitting.

But think before you quit. You can carry the love of Jesus to others. Without that love, you have no way of eternal life. Without that love you cannot help others.

If you leave the picnic basket behind, you have no lunch. If you leave Christ behind, you have no love and forgiveness from the one who died for you.

# Which Prophet Will You Believe?

**THE WORD:**

Jeremiah said, "The prophets who spoke long ago, before my time and yours, predicted that war, starvation, and disease would come to many nations and powerful kingdoms. But a prophet who predicts peace can only be recognized as a prophet whom the Lord has truly sent when that prophet's predictions come true."

Jeremiah 28:8-9 (Sixth Sunday after Pentecost)

**THE WORLD:**

A beautifully wrapped package with nothing in it and a brown paper bag with a gift suitable for the children.

Look at these two packages. Suppose I told you that one of them was a gift for you. Which would you choose? One looks like a better gift than the other. But I should warn you that looks can be deceiving. Let's peek. First, the fancy box. There's nothing in it. Now the brown sack. Look—it has a toy that you'd like to play with. The lesson is: You can't choose a gift by its wrapping.

Remember that lesson as we talk about our Bible reading for today. It tells us about two prophets. The first prophet is Jeremiah. God sent him to tell the people to change their ways. The people had forgotten God. They worshiped idols. They didn't care about each other. God had sent other prophets to tell them that unless they changed their ways, their nation would be destroyed. Now God sent Jeremiah to tell the people that they had to repent and change their ways.

The other man's name was Hananiah. He also claimed to be a prophet. Hananiah said that Jeremiah was wrong.

He said the people would have peace and health. Everything was going to be great.

The people had a choice. Hananiah offered them a happy message. But his prophecy was like this box *(fancy box)*. It was empty. God had not given Hananiah the message. Hananiah just told the people what they wanted to hear.

Jeremiah's message was like this *(the bag)*. It didn't look good. The people didn't want to hear it. But in those warnings God also gave a promise. God promised that he would stay with his people and bring them back. But the people chose the wrong prophet. They listened to Hananiah and missed God's gift.

You also have to choose between two messages. Many people will tell you that you don't have to go to church or read the Bible. Just do what you want to do and you'll be okay. That's like a fancy box with nothing in it.

But Jesus tells us that we are to follow him. He says we are to believe in him, hear his word, serve him, worship him. Sometimes we don't want to do those things. His gift sounds like work. It's like the sack. But remember what Jesus offers to those who believe in him and follow him. He forgives their sins. He loves them. He promises to be with them. He offers to take them to heaven.

Don't listen just to what you want to hear. Listen to what God has to say. He wants to tell you he loves you.

# How Do I Know for Sure?

**THE WORD:**

The Lord says, "Because of my covenant with you that was sealed by the blood of sacrifices, I will set your people free—free from the waterless pit of exile."

Zechariah 9:11 (Seventh Sunday after Pentecost)

**THE WORLD:**

Papers from a rental service and a twenty dollar bill.

Suppose you need a tent for a camping trip. Your father says he will rent one for you. Your father takes you to the store and signs this paper which says you will bring back the tent. But the rental service wants to know for sure that you will bring back the tent. So he asks for a deposit. Your father gives the store this (money).

You take the tent. The store keeps the twenty dollars. When you give the tent back, you get the deposit back. That way the store owner is sure you will bring it back.

You and I are like that store owner. God has said he loves us. He wants us to be with him. He tells us that in the Bible. We could say the Bible is like the papers your father signed when he rented the tent. The papers said he would bring the tent back. The Bible says God loves us.

But the man who rented the tent to you wanted to be sure that you would bring it back. He asked for a deposit. We want to be sure that God does love us. We need to know that God has forgiven our sins. In a way, we want a deposit from God.

God also wants us to be sure of his love. So he offers us a deposit. Listen to what God said through Zechariah in our Bible reading for today: "Because of my covenant with you that was sealed by the blood of sacrifices I will set your people free—free from the waterless pit of exile."

For the Old Testament people the deposit was the blood of sacrifices. The people would kill animals to show they knew they were sinners and sin would bring death. Each sacrifice was a reminder that God had promised to forgive their sins. The blood of the sacrifices were like a deposit to show that God would save the people.

We live in New Testament times. Jesus died to pay for our sins. He is God's deposit for us. He seals the promise God made to us.

You can be sure that God loves you. You can be sure your sins are forgiven. The Bible tells you this message. But you have more than words in a book. You have the fact that Jesus died for you. God gave his Son to die for us so we can be sure that he loves us. We can be sure our sins are forgiven, because Jesus died to take our punishment.

You can be sure God loves you, because God gave Jesus to be your Savior.

# The Word in the World

**THE WORD:**

> The Lord says, "My word is like the snow and the rain that come down from the sky to water the earth. They make the crops grow and provide seed for planting and food to eat. So also will be the word that I speak—it will not fail to do what I plan for it; it will do everything I send it to do."
>
> Isaiah 55:10-11 (Eighth Sunday after Pentecost)

**THE WORLD:**

> A healthy potted plant and a sickly or dead potted plant. (A branch from a healthy plant may be broken off the day before and stuck in dry soil.)

In our Bible reading God says, "My word is like the snow and the rain that come down from the sky to water the earth." Maybe you can't think of God's word as being like water. God's word isn't wet. You can't pour it. You can't drink it. You can't wash your face in it.

But God explains how his word is like the rain and snow. He says, "They make the crops grow and provide seed for planting and food to eat." Look at this plant *(healthy one)*. See, how green and fresh it is. Now look at this one *(sickly one)*. See, it is either dead or dying. Do you know what the difference is? The healthy one received water. The other did not. Feel the soil in the pot with the healthy plant. Now feel the dry soil in this pot. The water does something to the plant. It keeps the plant alive. It makes it grow.

What water does for the plant, God's word does for us. He says, "So also will be the word that I speak—it will not fail to do what I plan for it; it will do everything I send it to do."

God gives us his word for a purpose. In his word he tells us he loves us. He tells us that Jesus came to be our Savior by dying for our sins. God tells us that Jesus rose from the dead and because he lives we will live also. He tells us he is with us and cares for us. He tells us we will live with him forever.

God tells us that his word has power. It is his power to save all who believe. When we receive his word we are like a plant that is watered. We live spiritually. We grow spiritually. We produce spiritually.

Without God's word we cannot have a spiritual life. Our bodies can still be healthy. Without the word we can get good grades in school and have money. But our friendship with God cannot be healthy if we do not receive his word.

Think of yourself as a plant. When you are in church and when you read the Bible, you are being watered. You can grow and be strong in Jesus. If you feel your faith getting weak, remember you need the word of God to give you strength. Receive the word like a nice rain.

# God Has a Purpose

**THE WORD:**
God asks, "Could anyone else have done what I did?"
Isaiah 44:7a (Ninth Sunday after Pentecost)

**THE WORLD:**
Picture of a cookie, recipe book, dictionary, and a cookie.

Let's learn something about cookies. First, do you know what a cookie is? Sure you do, but let's look it up in the dictionary. This one says a cookie is, "a small, flat, sweet cake." Here is a picture of a cookie. What kind is it? Do you think it would taste good?

If you want to make cookies, you need a recipe book like this. It gives recipes for many kinds of cookies. Here's one for chocolate chip, oatmeal cookies, and sugar cookies. It's fun to look through a recipe book and think about all the different kinds of cookies.

You can learn about cookies by looking up the definition of cookie in the dictionary, by looking at a picture of a cookie and by reading recipes. But you still don't have a cookie. Only when you have this *(the cookie)* can you taste and enjoy the cookie. A cookie is for eating. You can't eat a definition, a picture, or a recipe. But you can eat a cookie.

But I am not interested in teaching you about cookies. I talked about cookies to help you understand something important about God. What do you know about God? This dictionary defines God like this: "The maker and ruler of the world; Supreme Being."

I can't show you a picture of God, but we use symbols to remind us of him. *(Point out some of the symbols in the worship area.)* The Bible tells us about God. It tells us who he is and what he has done. But it is not God. We use the Bible so we can know God. In today's Bible reading God asks us, "Could anyone else have done what I did?"

God has a purpose. He wants us to know him by knowing what he has done. Just as the cookie was made to be eaten, God exists to do things that only God can do.

Can anyone other than God create life? There is only one God who has made you and all people. Some people make gods out of the things that the true God has created. But only the one true God can create all things.

Only one God has offered to become one of us. He sent his Son Jesus to share in our lives. Jesus suffered with us. He was tempted with us. He even died for us. No other God has died to pay for our sins.

Then Jesus came back from the dead and promised us that we also can come back to life after we die. He has told us he will take us to heaven with him. No other God can give us such a promise.

That's why we want you to know God. Don't just know there is a God. Don't think of God as being far away up in heaven—or always waiting for you in a building. God is the one who loves you. No one else can love you like God has loved you. That's God's purpose—to love you.

# Ask God to
# Help You Help Yourself

**THE WORD:**

The Lord was pleased that Solomon had asked for this, and so he said to him, "Because you have asked for the wisdom to rule justly, instead of a long life for yourself or riches or the death of your enemies, I will do what you have asked. I will give you more wisdom and understanding than anyone has ever had before or will ever have again."

1 Kings 3:10-12 (Tenth Sunday after Pentecost)

**THE WORLD:**

A five dollar bill and material for washing windows.

Jason and Seth wanted to go to the fair. But they knew it would cost them at least five dollars each. And they were broke. So they decided to ask their parents for the money.

Jason ran home and said, "Hey, Mom, can I have five dollars? I want to go to the fair. His mother said no. She said he received an allowance and should have saved some of his own money.

Seth ran home and said, "I need some extra money for the fair. Do you have a job I could do to earn five bucks?" His mother said he could wash the windows. She gave him this equipment to do the job. In a few hours he was through. She gave him the five dollars.

Each boy asked his mother for help. But they asked in a different way. Jason asked for five dollars. Seth asked for a way to earn five dollars. Seth received what he asked for. He was like Solomon in our Bible reading. God asked Solomon what he wanted. Solomon could have asked God to do his job for him. He could have asked God to get rid

90

of his enemies, give him lots of money and make him a good king.

Instead Solomon asked God to give him wisdom so he could be a good king. He needed wisdom to get rid of his enemies. He needed wisdom to make his country wealthy. God told Solomon that if he had been like Jason and asked him to do the work, God would have said no. But Solomon was like Seth. He asked God to help him do his work. He knew he needed God's help. But he also knew he had to do something himself.

God has also invited you to ask him for help. How do you pray to God? Do you ask God to do everything for you? Or do you ask God to help you do what you should do? Do you ask God to give you good grades in school; or do you ask God to help you study to get good grades? Do you ask God to make you the best player of all; or do you ask God to help you practice hard and play well? Do you ask God to give you money, or do you ask him to make you a good worker?

God wants to give you every blessing. He even gave you his Son to be your Savior. If Christ was willing to die for you, you know God wants to give you everything you need. But God wants to let you share in the good things of your life. He created you so you could do things for yourself and for others. You still need his help. But instead of doing them for you, he helps you do many things.

Ask God for help every time you need it. But also listen to his answer. His answer may be to tell you how you can help get what you need.

# Buy Without Money

**THE WORD:**

The Lord says, "Come, everyone who is thirsty—here is water! Come, you that have no money—buy grain and eat! Come! Buy wine and milk—it will cost you nothing!"
Isaiah 55:1 (Eleventh Sunday after Pentecost)

**THE WORLD:**

A Frisbee and a child's billfold filled with pictures, ID, etc., and a credit card, but no money.

---

Suppose you are walking through a shopping center past a booth that is selling frisbees. The sales clerk calls out to you, "Come and buy a frisbee here."

You answer, "I have no money." See, this is your billfold. Not a dime. Just pictures and papers, but no money.

What if the sales clerk said, "But you can buy without money"? You know you can't buy anything without money. Yet listen to what God says in the Bible reading for today, "Come, everyone who is thirsty—here is water! Come you that have no money—buy grain and eat! Come! Buy wine and milk—it will cost you nothing!"

Sounds like a contradiction, doesn't it? God does not say, "Come and get it for free." He says, "Come and buy!" But he also says that you do not need money. God is not offering to sell you a frisbee. He wants you to have love, forgiveness, freedom, peace, joy, eternal life. Those are the most important things in life. So important that you can't buy them with money. Yet so expensive that they must be earned. So how are you going to get them?

Let's go back to the clerk at the frisbee counter. You said you could not buy the toy because you had no money. But the clerk said you could buy it without money —because you have this (the credit card). This is your parents' credit card and they told you that you may use it to buy the frisbee. You still have no money. But you can buy the frisbee. You buy it on your parents' credit.

Now listen to the offer God makes to you. He wants to help you. He wants you to have those things we talked about—love, forgiveness, freedom, joy, eternal life. He tells you to buy them without money, because they can't be bought with money. They cost too much.

But they have been bought. Jesus Christ died for you. He paid the price of his own life so you could have the great spiritual blessings that God wants you to have. You can buy them by charging them to Jesus Christ. He lets you use his credit card to pay for the spiritual needs of your life.

These blessings are not free. They were paid for by Jesus Christ. Now he gives them to you. You can't pay for them, because he already has paid the price. Now he offers them to you. Come buy love and forgiveness—it will cost you nothing. Buy joy and eternal life—it will cost you nothing.

# You Are Not Alone

**THE WORD:**
Elijah said, "I am the only one left—and they are trying to kill me." . . . The Lord said, "Yet I will leave seven thousand people alive in Israel—all those who are loyal to me and have not bowed to Baal or kissed his idol."
1 Kings 19:14b and 18 (Twelfth Sunday after Pentecost)
**THE WORLD:**
A pair of children's socks.

Have you ever looked in your dresser drawer and found only one sock? *(Show a single sock.)* If you are getting ready for school and have only one sock and two feet, you have a problem. You might as well have no socks as to have only one. You can't wear one sock.

Elijah felt like a single sock. God had called him to be a prophet. Elijah told the people to stop worshiping idols. He had even told King Ahab and Queen Jezebel to repent. Instead of repenting, Jezebel sent the palace police out to kill Elijah.

Elijah had to hide in a wilderness. He was all alone. He had no family—no friends. No one listened to his message from God. He felt like a single sock—worthless. He said, "I am the only one left—and they are trying to kill me." He thought he was the only one left who loved God. And he was ready to die.

You can understand how Elijah felt. What would you do with a lone sock? Throw it away? Your mother might say, "No, you don't throw it away. You look for the other sock." So you look in the clothes hamper and you find this *(second sock)*. Now you have a pair for school. You are glad you didn't throw the first one away.

94

When Elijah told God he was the only one left so he might as well die, God said, "No, you're not alone. I will leave seven thousand people alive in Israel—all those who are loyal to me and have not bowed to Baal or kissed his idol."

Elijah was not alone. Seven thousand others also loved God. Maybe each of the others also felt alone. Elijah had to go on sharing the message of God; so the others would know they were not alone.

Have you ever felt like a single sock? You might think you are the only Christian in your class, or on your team, or living on your block or in your apartment house. When you think you are the only one left you might also think you should give up. Some people give up and never talk about Jesus. They use bad words so others will not know they are Christian.

But God tells you: You are not alone. My son Jesus died for all people. I love all of your classmates, all the kids on your team, all the people on your block or in your apartment house. And some of them love me too. You are not alone. Show your faith in Jesus so others will know you love him. Then they will see your faith and they can show you they are Christian too.

# One Size Fits All

**THE WORD:**

The Lord says, "My Temple will be called a house of prayer for the people of all nations."

Isaiah 56:7b (Thirteenth Sunday after Pentecost)

**THE WORLD:**

A cross worn as a pin by the speaker. (If in vestments, wear the cross on the stole.)

Would any of you be willing to trade shoes with me? I'll wear your shoes and you wear mine. *(Either take off shoes and compare sizes or place feet side by side to show the difference.)* I guess we can't trade shoes. Mine are too big for you. And yours are too small for me.

Am I wearing anything that would fit you? *(If in vestments ask: "Could you wear this alb? Here, try on my stole.")* You couldn't wear my belt, or my shirt, or my pants. And I couldn't wear your clothes either. Our clothes come in different sizes. Some people wear the same size. *(Compare two children who are about the same size.)* But we need many sizes of clothes because there are many sizes of people.

But I am wearing something that would fit each of you. Not only would it fit all of you, it would fit any person in the whole world. Can you see what I am wearing that would fit you? See this—it's a cross. It fits me. And it also fits you *(hold the cross up to several children)*. One size fits all.

I chose the cross as an example of something that would fit everyone because the cross reminds us of Jesus who loves all people. Jesus fits all people because he forgives sin. All need his forgiveness. Jesus fits all because he died for us. All of us will die. Jesus will share our death. Jesus rose from the dead. He promises to raise all people from the dead and take those who believe in him to heaven. What Jesus gives us is in the right size to fit all of us.

We who believe in Jesus are the church today. That means we are to do what he wants done. But do we have a church that has one size to fit all? Or is our church like our clothes. Do we make some people think they don't fit in our church? Listen to what the Bible reading for today tells us: The Lord says, "My Temple will be called a house of prayer for the people of all nations." This should also be true of the church.

The Christian church is based on the life and teachings of Jesus Christ who came to be the Savior of the world. He is not for only one kind or class of people. While he was on earth Jesus showed that he came for people of all races, for men and women, for children and all people, for rich and poor. Jesus is the Savior for all people. We as a church must also be for all people.

# God by Another Name Is Lord

**THE WORD:**

God spoke to Moses and said, "I am the Lord. I appeared to Abraham, to Isaac, and to Jacob as Almighty God, but I did not make myself known to them by my holy name, the Lord."

Exodus 6:2-3 (Fourteenth Sunday after Pentecost)

**THE WORLD:**

Salt—in a box or bag as it comes from the store.

---

What store would you go to if you wanted to buy apples? A grocery store or a fruit stand, right? Where would you buy a pair of socks? At a department store or a clothing store. Where would you buy sodium chloride? Can you say those words? *(Help the children pronounce sodium chloride.)* Sounds like something you might buy at a drug store. But that's not the easiest place to get it. First, you have to know what sodium chloride is. Let me show you.

This is sodium chloride. *(Show salt.)* It's salt. You know where to buy salt. At the grocery store, right? If you know the easy name for sodium chloride you have no problem pronouncing it and you know where to buy it.

Like salt, many other things have a difficult name and an easy name. Even God has more than one title to describe him. Listen to what he says to Moses in the Bible lesson for today, "I am the Lord. I appeared to Abraham, to Isaac, and to Jacob as the Almighty God, but I did not make myself known to them by my holy name, the Lord."

Abraham, Isaac, and Jacob knew God as the Almighty God. That is a good name for him. It reminds us of his power and greatness. But God wanted Moses to know him by an easier name. He said to Moses, "I am the Lord." A Lord is one who has power and authority. But a Lord also has love and concern. The name Lord reminds us of both the power of God and the love of God. God wanted Moses to know he had the power to help the people of Israel escape from Egypt. He also wanted Moses to know that he loved all the people and wanted to help them. So he invited Moses to call him Lord.

We know God by both of his names, Almighty God and Lord. We also know him as Jesus Christ. God sent his Son Jesus to be our Savior. We know Jesus as the One who lived on earth, who healed people, who taught people how to live in love and forgiveness. We know him as the one who died for our sins. We know him as the one who rose from the dead and opened the door to heaven for all who believe in him.

We call Jesus Lord because we see both power and love in him. Through Jesus we know God. We can see God as the Almighty God without being afraid of him, because we also see him as the one who sent Jesus to be our Savior.

Be glad that God has let you see him as Lord. Be glad that you can know God because you know Jesus is your Lord and Savior.

# Forgiveness for One—and All

**THE WORD:**

Then I (Jeremiah) said, "Lord, you understand. Remember me and help me. Let me have revenge on those who persecute me. . . ." To this the Lord replied, "If you return, I will take you back, and you will be my servant again. If instead of talking nonsense you proclaim a worthwhile message, you will be my prophet again."

Jeremiah 15:15a, 19a (Fifteenth Sunday after Pentecost)

**THE WORLD:**

A stack of homework by primary students.

Seth's mother was late in picking him up from school one day. His teacher let Seth stay in the classroom and asked him to help sort homework; so she could grade it. She gave him this stack of papers. She told Seth to stack the papers neatly.

When Seth looked at Jennifer's paper he saw it was messy. *(Point out smudges on the paper.)* So he told the teacher Jennifer should do the work over. Then he said that Billy's paper was not finished; so he should do it over. Seth found something wrong with each paper.

Then he came to his own paper. He gave it to the teacher. The teacher said, "Look at your paper, Seth. It has a smudge on it. It is not finished. Don't you think you should do it over?"

"But I tried hard," answered Seth. "I did not have time to finish it. Someone bumped me and made the mess on the paper."

Seth found an excuse for all the mistakes he had made. But he did not understand why the others made mistakes. Jeremiah did the same thing in our Bible reading. He

100

asked God to help him punish other people who had done wrong. God told Jeremiah he was talking nonsense. God said Jeremiah should say something worthwhile. If Jeremiah wanted God to love and forgive him when he was wrong, then Jeremiah would also have to love and forgive others when they were wrong.

Do you make the same mistake that Seth and Jeremiah made? Do you find fault with others? Do you always see the mistakes your brothers and sisters make, but not your own? Do you want to tell the teacher each time one of the other kids at school does something wrong, but do you want no one to know when you do something wrong? Do you like to see others punished for their mistakes?

God does forgive you. He sent Jesus Christ to be your Savior. When Jesus died for you he took away all your sin. But God also sent Jesus for all other people. Jesus also died for all others. All people may receive the same forgiveness from Jesus that you have.

God said that Jeremiah was talking nonsense when the prophet wanted to punish others. Then God invited Jeremiah to share his message for all people. God does not ask you to find fault with others and to punish them. Instead he lets you share the love and forgiveness he has given you with all others who need that same love and forgiveness.

# Pass the Message On

**THE WORD:**

> The Lord said, "If I announce that an evil man is going to die but you do not warn him to change his ways so that he can save his life, then he will die, still a sinner, and I will hold you responsible for his death. If you do warn an evil man and he doesn't stop sinning, he will die still a sinner, but your life will be spared."
>
> Ezekiel 38:8-9 (Sixteenth Sunday after Pentecost)

**THE WORLD:**

Two job lists.

Stacey and Kelley are sisters. Their mother had to go to work on Saturday. Before she left she made two lists of chores she wanted the girls to do. *(Show the lists.)* This is Stacey's list and this is Kelley's.

Since Stacey is the older, the mother gave both lists to her and said, "Do all the chores on your list and give this list to Kelley."

But Stacey did not give the list to her sister. Kelley did not do the chores she was supposed to do. When the mother came home she saw the work was not done. Whose fault was it? Stacey's, of course. She did not give the list to Kelley; so Kelley did not know what she was supposed to do.

If Stacey would have given the list to her sister and Kelley had not done the work, then it would have been Kelley's fault that she did not do the chores.

Think about Stacey and Kelley and listen to what God told Ezekiel, "If I announce that an evil man is going to die but you do not warn him to change his ways so that he can save his life, then he will die, still a sinner, and I will hold you responsible for his death. If you do warn an evil man and he doesn't stop sinning, he will die, still a sinner, but your life will be spared."

We also are to warn people about their sins. But we have more than a warning to give. We also have good news. Jesus has died for our sins. He has taken our punishment for us. We are forgiven.

If we do not warn people about their sins and tell them that Jesus is their Savior they will not know that they need forgiveness and they will not know that Jesus wants to forgive them. They will be like Kelley—they won't get the message. Then it is our fault that they do not know Jesus as their Savior, because we didn't tell them.

That does not mean that we can make people believe in Jesus. All we can do is warn them about their sins and tell them about the love of Jesus. If they have heard and do not believe, it is not our fault.

Be glad that you have not only a warning to give but also the good news that Jesus is the Savior. Many people do not know that Jesus died to pay for their sins. You can be the one who passes the message on.

# Good Can Come from Evil

**THE WORD:**

> But Joseph said to them (his brothers), "Don't be afraid; I can't put myself in the place of God. You plotted evil against me, but God turned it into good, in order to preserve the lives of many people who are alive today because of what happened."
>
> Genesis 50:19-20 (Seventeenth Sunday after Pentecost)

**THE WORLD:**

A book bag, several textbooks, some magazines.

Kris was a good student. Each afternoon he put his books in his book bag *(do it)* to take them home to study. Some of his friends were jealous because Kris got good grades. One afternoon while Kris was getting a drink of water they took his books out of the bag and filled it with magazines. *(Do it.)* Kris took the book bag and went home.

On the way home Kris lost his book bag. He thought he had lost all of his schoolbooks. But when he got to school the next day he found his books in his desk. The other boys had intended to hurt him. Instead they helped him. All he lost were his book bag and old magazines.

Something like that happened to Joseph in the Old Testament. His brothers were jealous of him; so they sold him to be a slave in Egypt. God told Joseph there would be dry weather and no food. Joseph told the king who asked Joseph to help him store up grain for the time when there would be no crops. When others were out of food the Egyptians ate the food they had saved. Even Joseph's brothers came to Egypt for food. When they saw Joseph they were afraid. But Joseph said, "Don't be afraid; I can't put myself in the place of God. You plotted evil against me, but God turned it into good."

Joseph's brothers were wrong when they sold him as a slave. The boys who took Kris' books were wrong. But God can make something good happen even when we do wrong.

God's love and power are so great that he can make good things happen to us even when we do bad things. That does not mean that good always comes from evil. When you do bad things you hurt yourself and others. But God can help you. When you do something bad, remember God still loves you. Jesus died for you while you were still a sinner. He wants to take away your sin and give you his love.

If your sin makes you feel sorry and turn to Jesus for help, then something good has happened. Your sin made you know you need Jesus. You see him as your Savior. You ask him to forgive what you have done wrong and to help you not do it again. You know Jesus is with you and helps you. Even though you sinned something good came from it because you came closer to your Savior.

Don't ever sin on purpose so God can make good come from bad. Instead, let God help you do good. But when you do something wrong, don't hide from God. Remember he still loves you. He can make good come from something bad.

# Our Way and God's Way

**THE WORD:**

> "My thoughts," says the Lord, "are not like yours, and my ways are different from yours. As high as the heavens are above the earth, so high are my ways and thoughts above yours."
>
> Isaiah 55:8-9 (Eighteenth Sunday after Pentecost)

**THE WORLD:**

A typewriter, paper, and a person who can type well.

Do any of you know how to type? Let's see if you can type your name. *(Help one or two of the children type. Show them how to make a capital letter and how to space.)* One way to type is to find each letter you want and strike that key.

But there is another way. *(Have someone who types well type several lines.)* Now that's another way to type. One way is to find each key, one at a time. The other way is to know the keys so well that you don't even have to think about them. A person who types well just thinks the words and automatically hits the right keys.

God tells us there are also two ways to think. There's the human way—that's the way you and I think. Then there is God's way to think. In our Bible reading God says, "My thoughts are not like yours and my ways are different from yours. As high as the heavens are above the earth, so high are my ways and thoughts above yours."

God thinks in a much higher way than we do. He does things in a better way than we do. He is not telling us we are stupid. God gave us our minds and we can do great and wonderful things with our brains. But we cannot think like God. We are people so we think like people. And that's okay. We can't even pretend we are God and think like him. Let's talk about some of the ways that God thinks in a different way than we do:

First, when we think, we always think about ourselves first, then the people we love. We don't care about some people and we don't even know many more people. That's the human way. But think about God's way. God does not think about himself first. If Jesus had thought only about himself he would not have died on the cross. But he thought about all people. His thoughts are higher than ours. He can care for all people. He died to pay for everyone's sin. He wants to give the blessing of his victory over death to all people. That's how God thinks.

Second, we think we have to earn what we get. According to our human way of thinking, if we work hard we get paid a lot. If we are lazy and do little, we get little. If we do right we will be rewarded. If we do wrong, we will be punished. All of that is correct according to the human way of thinking.

But God thinks in a different way. Instead of making us earn what he has for us, he gives his gifts to us. He does not offer to take us to heaven because we deserve it, but because he loves us and wants us there. According to his way of thinking we can depend on him and he will take care of us.

In our way of thinking we have to serve God. In his way of thinking we can serve him because we love him.

# The Right Way
# and the Wrong Way

**THE WORD:** •

"But you say, 'What the Sovereign Lord does isn't right.'
Listen to me, you Israelites. You think my way of doing
things isn't right? It is your way that isn't right . . . Give
up all the evil you have been doing, and get yourselves
new minds and hearts. Why do you Israelites want to die?
I do not want you to die," says the Sovereign Lord, "Turn
away from your sin and live."
Ezekiel 18:25, 31-32 (Nineteenth Sunday after Pentecost)

**THE WORLD:**
Several sheets of colored paper, scissors.

Do you know the easy way to cut out a heart like we
use on valentines? Fold a piece of paper in half, like this.
Then cut half a heart *(do it, but cut from the open side)*.
Then you have this *(show the two pieces)*. That shows
there is a wrong way to do everything. There is also a
right way. See *(fold paper and cut from the folded side)*.
See—now I have a heart. It's easy to do if you know the
right way.

In our Bible reading God says that some people tell him
he does things the wrong way. They said he was wrong
because he punished people for sin. But God says he is not
wrong. He says we are wrong. He tells us to look at the
way we do things and the way he does things. Which is
right? If you keep on doing something the wrong way, it
will never become right just because you do it that way.
If you keep trying to make a heart by cutting from the
open end of a folded paper, it will never turn out right.

If you keep on sinning, the sin will never become good.
It will always be wrong. So God says we are wrong if we

blame him. Instead we should give up our sin. He wants us to stop doing what is wrong. You have to admit you are wrong before you can stop it. If you argued that this is the way *(wrong way)* to cut a heart, you will never learn the right way.

When we sin we punish ourselves. Our sin hurts us and others. God asks us why we keep on sinning. He wonders, "Why do you want to die?"

God says, "I do not want anyone to die. Turn away from your sins and live." God wants all of us to be in heaven with him. God also shows us a way to heaven even though we have sinned. Jesus came to be our Savior. He tells us that he is the way of eternal life.

When God tells us to give up all the evil we do, he invites us to give the evil to Jesus. Jesus has paid the price of our sin by his suffering and death. We need to repent every day and give our sins to Jesus. Then Jesus gives us his love and forgiveness.

There's a right way and a wrong way to do everything. When things go wrong, don't blame God. His ways are right and ours are wrong. But part of his way of doing things is to give us his rightness in Jesus Christ.

# What Does God Expect of You?

**THE WORD:**

Israel is the vineyard of the Lord Almighty; the people of Judah are the vines he planted. He expected them to do what was good, but instead they committed murder. He expected them to do what was right, but their victims cried out for justice.

Isaiah 5:7 (Twentieth Sunday after Pentecost)

**THE WORLD:**

A container of spoiled milk—either keep the milk at room temperature for several days or add vinegar to it so it will smell bad.

Let's suppose you are eating lunch at school and you have this container of milk on your tray. You look forward to drinking the milk because it tastes good, it is healthful, and you are thirsty. But when you open it, it smells bad. See: *(let several children smell the milk)*. It is spoiled. You can't drink it. You are disappointed.

Isaiah says God is often disappointed in his people, just as you were disappointed in the milk. God expects us to do what is good, and what is right. Instead we often do what is wrong and bad. You expected the milk to be good, but it was spoiled.

God created us to be his people. He wanted us to be like him. He wanted us to love all the other people. He wanted us to enjoy being with him. We disappoint God when we do not do what he expects. We disappoint him when we hurt ourselves or others. We disappoint him when we hide from him and refuse to listen to him or talk to him.

We can use the spoiled milk to understand something about God. We can see how we are like God. We are disappointed when something doesn't turn out like we expected. We are hurt when something we wanted to be good turns out to be bad. God feels the same way.

But we can also see how we are different from God. What do you think I will do with this spoiled milk? That's right. I will throw it away. It is no good anymore. I don't want to keep it because it does not smell good.

But that is not what God does. He is disappointed in us. We have not done what he expected us to do. But he does not throw us away. He does not give up on us. He does not destroy us.

Instead he sent Jesus to make us good again. There is no way I can make the milk good again. It is spoiled. But God found a way to make us good again. He sent Jesus to be good in our place. When Jesus lived a good life he did the good things we had failed to do. When Jesus died on the cross he paid for all the wrong we had done.

God was not disappointed in Jesus. He tells us he was pleased with him. Jesus was the kind of person God had made all of us to be. Now God lets us have the credit for what Jesus did. Because Jesus is our Savior he will not throw us away even though we have not done what he expected us to do.

Now that Jesus is our Savior we can do many of the things God expected us to do. We can love and serve God. We can love and forgive other people. God keeps us for a purpose. With Jesus we can do what he expects us to do.

# When Do You Say "Thanks God"?

**THE WORD:**

The Sovereign Lord will destroy death forever! He will wipe away the tears from everyone's eyes and take away the disgrace his people have suffered throughout the world. The Lord himself has spoken. When it happens, everyone will say, "He is our God! We have put our trust in him and he has rescued us. He is the Lord! We have put our trust in him, and now we are happy and joyful because he has saved us."

Isaiah 25:8-9 (Twenty-first Sunday after Pentecost)

**THE WORLD:**

A check in a gift envelope, and 25 dollars in cash.

Think about one of your uncles. If you don't have an uncle, think about an older friend—someone who likes you and is good to you. Suppose that person says, "I am going to give you a check for $25.00."

When are you going to say, "Thank you" for the gift? You could say thanks when he tells you that he is going to give you the gift. Or you could wait until he hands you this *(the envelope)*. Or you could wait until you cash the check and get this *(cash)*.

The time you choose to say thank you shows how much you trust the uncle. Do you believe him when he says he will give you the gift? Then you thank him when he makes the promise. Do you think his check is good—that he has the money in the bank? Then you thank him when he gives you the check. But if you really don't trust the uncle, you'd better wait until you have the cash in your hand.

The Bible reading for today tells about a promise—not from an uncle, but from God. The promise is this: "The

Sovereign Lord will destroy death forever! He will wipe away the tears from everyone's eyes and take away the disgrace his people have suffered throughout the world. The Lord himself has spoken."

God made this promise through Isaiah over 700 years before Jesus was born. God promised to destroy death. When Jesus came he died on a cross. For a while it looked like death had destroyed Jesus, but three days later Jesus arose from the grave. He tells us that because he died and lives again we can also die and live again. Death has been destroyed. God will wipe away our tears and take away our disgrace.

When are you going to thank God for taking away the power of death? We are like the person who received the check—but had not cashed it. We have the gift of Jesus. We know he has come back from death. But we haven't died and come back yet. We are still waiting to cash in on that promise. If we trust God, we can thank him now. If not, we will have to wait until Judgment Day; when we see the Risen Lord.

God tells us that on the last day all will know he is the Lord. But we don't have to wait until then to enjoy our gift of life. Because we know and trust Jesus as our Savior, we can enjoy our new life now. We can thank God now for the gift that he has given us.

# One Person's Blessing
# —Another's Disaster

**THE WORD:**
> The Lord said, "I create both light and darkness; I bring both blessing and disaster. I, the Lord, do all these things."
> Isaiah 45:7 (Twenty-second Sunday after Pentecost)

**THE WORLD:**
A potted plant and a baseball bat.

---

Instead of seeing this as one little plant in a pot of soil see it as a big crop in a field. Instead of seeing this as just a baseball bat see it as an important ball game, with the balls, gloves, and two teams.

One more thing to pretend: the big field is next to the baseball diamond. The soil is dry. The farmer who owns the field prays for rain. The kids on the baseball team pray for a sunny day.

What does God do? He loves all people. He wants to help both the farmer and the ball players. The rain would be a blessing for the farmer and a disaster for the players. A sunny day would be a blessing for the ball game but a disaster for the farmer.

Listen to what God tells us in our Bible reading, "I create both light and darkness; I bring both blessings and disaster. I, the Lord, do all these things." We thank God for rain when we want rain. We also know that the rain comes from God even if we don't want it. A blessing at one time is a disaster at another.

God spoke these words to Cyrus, a king who was going to free his people who were slaves in another country. Cyrus would come with an army. The soldiers would kill some of the Israelites. The war would be a disaster for

114

them. But others would be made free by the same war—a blessing for them.

Sometimes our blessings are disasters for others. When you win a game, someone else loses. You have the blessing of more than enough to eat, but someone else has the disaster of not enough to eat. Your blessing is a disaster for someone else.

Sometimes a blessing for someone else will be a disaster for you. If someone else makes the team, or the choir or the honor roll, it may mean you won't make it. When you grow up someone else may get the job you want. A blessing for the other person, but a disaster for you.

But if you know God loves you, you can live with disasters and not be afraid. You can also accept blessings and not be proud. Jesus gives you that love so you can accept both blessing and disaster. Jesus had both disaster and blessing in his life. He had the disaster of suffering and death. But he also had the blessing of victory over death when he rose from the dead.

Jesus did those things for you and me. He did not take all of our disaster away. But he shares them with us. He helps us live through them. He also gives us blessings. And he lets us share those blessings with others.

# Give Love—Not Revenge

**THE WORD:**
> Do not take revenge on anyone or continue to hate him, but love your neighbor as you love yourself. I am the Lord.
> Leviticus 19:18 (Twenty-third Sunday after Pentecost)

**THE WORLD:**
> Two pictures drawn by children as an assignment, two crayons.

Suppose this is a picture you drew at school. The teacher is going to put the pictures on a wall for all to see. While your picture is on the teacher's desk another student puts his on top of yours. *(Drop the second picture on the first but not so they are even with one another.)* The other student writes his name on his picture. But his crayon goes off the edge of his picture and marks yours. *(Do it.)* Now look at your picture. When it is up on the wall, all will see the other mark.

When someone does something against us we sometimes want to get revenge, that means to get even. We think that if someone hurts us we have a right to hurt them in the same way. If someone else made a mark on your picture, you would have a right to make a mark on his picture. *(Do it.)* But he would say that his mark on yours was an accident. To get even with you, he would make another mark on your picture. *(Do it.)* To get even with him you would mark his; and he marks yours again. *(Do it.)* Soon both pictures are ruined.

Other people will often hurt you—sometimes accidentally and sometimes on purpose. But when you try to get even you will not only hurt the other person, you will also hurt yourself. Revenge is dangerous because it keeps a problem alive and makes it grow even bigger.

In our Bible reading God tells us not to get even with others when they hurt us. He says, "Do not take revenge on anyone or continue to hate him, but love your neighbor as you love yourself. I am the Lord."

God gives you two reasons why you should not try to get even with anyone. First he says you are to love your neighbor as you love yourself. You wanted your picture to look nice; so you should also want the other student's picture to look nice. You don't want to be hurt; so you should not want others to be hurt either.

When God tells us to love our neighbor as ourselves, he is reminding us that he loves all of us equally. When Jesus came to be our Savior, he came for all of us. He knows we all have done wrong, but he forgives us. He does not take sides when we hurt each other because he knows all of us have been hurt and all of us have hurt others. Instead he helps us by loving us and by giving us love for each other. The way to stop others from hurting us is to stop hurting them. If we love them they won't want to hurt us.

God gives us another reason not to get even with anyone who hurts us. He says, "I am the Lord." He is my Lord. He is your Lord. He is the Lord of the person who hurt you. If anyone needs to be punished it is his job to punish—not ours. Jesus our Lord took the punishment for all people when he died for us. He gave us love—not punishment. We can give love to others—not revenge.

# Don't Be Scared Any More

**THE WORD:**

How terrible it will be for you who long for the day of the Lord! What good will that day do you? For you it will be a day of darkness and not of light. It will be like a man who runs from a lion and meets a bear!

Amos 5:18-19a (Twenty-fourth Sunday after Pentecost)

**THE WORLD:**

Two items from a drugstore (appropriate for the age of the children involved), a bag from that store, and a sales slip.

One time a girl named Jean went to a drugstore. She saw this toy and wanted it. *(Show the toy.)* But she did not want to spend her money. So she put the toy under her coat and walked out of the store. No one noticed. The next week she was back in the store. Again she saw a toy she wanted. *(Show the second toy.)* She put it under her coat. She walked out of the door. But a clerk saw her and walked toward her. She started to run. But a store detective came from the other direction. She was trapped. They took her to the office and called her parents.

You can imagine how she felt when she was caught. The Old Testament prophet Amos said all people will feel caught on the day when God comes to judge the world. He says we will feel like a person who runs from a lion, only to meet a bear. On Judgment Day we will want to run from God because we know we have done wrong. But when we run from him we find ourselves running toward the devil. We will feel caught. That is scary.

Now let's finish the story about Jean. After she talked to her parents she realized she was wrong. She promised never to steal from the store again. Later she was in the same store. She saw these two toys *(same items)* and she bought them. The clerk gave her a sales slip and put the toys in the bag. As she walked out of the store she saw the clerk and the store detective. She remembered what happened before and was afraid. She started to run. Then she remembered! She didn't have to run. She had this. *(Show the sales slip.)* The toys she had were paid for. She could walk out of the store without being afraid.

Now let's talk about Judgment Day again. When God comes to judge the world, he is the same God who came first to save the world. He came to live here and then he died to pay for all of our sins. He gave us this *(sales slip)*. It shows he has paid for our sins. He paid the price. He gave the proof that he paid for us when he rose from the dead.

When Judgment Day comes, you don't have to run from God. You may remember that you have done wrong. But also remember that Jesus came to pay for your sins. He will come not to scare you, but to take you to heaven with him.

# Keep the Name Tags Straight

**THE WORD:**

God said, "Yet I was the one who taught Israel to walk. I took my people up in my arms, but they did not acknowledge that I took care of them. I drew them to me with affection and love. I picked them up and held them to my cheek; I bent down to them and fed them."

Hosea 11:3-4 (Twenty-fifth Sunday after Pentecost)

**THE WORLD:**

A science fair project, four large name tags (Bill, Tom, Jesus, Me), a bag of cookies.

Here is a story about two fourth graders, Tom and Bill. Their class had a science fair. Tom worked hard to collect leaves and made this project. He put his name on the collection. On the way to school Tom met Bill. Bill had forgotten to make a project for the fair. But Tom invited Bill to share in his project. So Bill carried the project to school. Bill put his name on the project too—right over the top of Tom's. *(Do it.)*

The judges picked Tom's project for a prize. But the teacher could only see Bill's name. So she gave the prize, this package of cookies, to Bill. Bill accepted the cookies without mentioning that Tom had done the work. Then Bill ate the cookies himself. He didn't give Tom any.

That's a sad story. We think Bill was a bad kid. If we were Tom, we would be very angry. But in our Bible reading the prophet Hosea tells us that people often treat God that way. We must ask ourselves if we are like Bill.

God is like Tom. He does the work. He has created us. He takes care of us. He came to be our Savior and to suffer and die for our sins. He offers us a place to live with him forever. When Jesus saves us, he puts his name on us. *(Put the tag "Jesus" on yourself.)*

But often we are like Bill. We take the gifts from God and put our name on top. *(Put "Me" over "Jesus".)* We take the gifts that God has offered us and act as though they were our own. Sometimes we refuse to give even a part of what God has given us back to him. We are like Bill when we accept all the gifts God has for us but do not give him credit, do not thank him and do not serve him. In our Bible reading God says, "I was the one who taught Israel to walk. I took my people up in my arms, but they did not acknowledge that I took care of them."

But God did not hate the people for being selfish. He did not leave them. Listen to what he did instead, "I drew them to me with affection and love. I picked them up and held them to my cheek; I bent down to them and fed them."

God keeps on loving us. He holds us close to him so we can feel his love. When we put ourselves in front of him *(show name tags)*, he does not leave us. Instead he keeps loving us. He wants us to remember what he has done for us. When we remember him and feel his love, we want to put his name in front. But he says, "No." He wants to share in our lives. He wants our name beside his. He invites us to share in all he has done for us.

# Help Me Be a Good Teacher

**THE WORD:**

God said, "They (priests) taught what was right, not what was wrong. They lived in harmony with me; they not only did what was right themselves, but they also helped many others to stop doing evil."

Malachi 2:6 (Twenty-sixth Sunday after Pentecost)

**THE WORLD:**

Three flash cards as follows: 2x3 = 6, 3x5 = 15, 4x6 = 28 (For young children, use simple addition; for older, use more complicated multiplication.)

Do you ever think of me as your teacher? I know you have other teachers. You have a teacher in school and a Sunday school teacher. But I am also teacher when you come here and we share God's Word together.

The word that we share today tells how important it is that I teach you the truth from God's Word. It is also important that you learn the truth God gives you. Listen to what God said through the prophet Malachi, "They, that is the priests, taught what was right, not what was wrong. They lived in harmony with me; they not only did what was right themselves, but they also helped many others to stop doing evil."

But the people did not always have such good priests. Later on Malachi tells us that some of the priests taught the people wrong things. Instead of teaching what God said, they taught their own ideas. Let's see what would happen if you learned something that is not true. In math class you may learn to multiply with flash cards like these.

What is 2 times 3? *(Show card.)* See, the card shows you the answer. What is 3 times 5? *(Show card.)* Again the card helps you check yourself to see if you know the answer. What is 4 times 6? *(Show card.)* What is the answer? Did you notice the answer on the card is wrong? If you learned 4 times 6 is 28, you are wrong. Until you learned the right answer, you would be wrong each time you multiplied 4 times 6. That could cause you problems all of your life on earth.

But you would have an even greater problem if you learned wrong things about God. Let's check some things you know about God.

Do you know that God sent Jesus to be your Savior? Jesus became a person like us so he could die for us. He rose from the dead so he could also bring us back to life after we die. Some people think Jesus is only a teacher, or just a good person. But I want to teach you that he is your Savior and that he loves you very much.

Do you know what to do when you sin? Some people hide their sin. Some try to defend what they do wrong and say it makes no difference. Others just try to forget about their sin. But Jesus tells you to ask him to forgive your sin. He wants to forgive you. That's why he died for you. He took the punishment for your sin.

We could talk about many other things that God wants to teach you. That's why I like to be here with you each Sunday. Other people teach me the truth about God's love in Jesus Christ and I am glad I can teach you that same message.

I want to be a good teacher like those God talked about in our Bible reading. I want you to be good learners like those people were. You help me be a good teacher and I'll do my best to help you be good learners.

# Read the Instructions, Before You Fail

**THE WORD:**

I, the Lord, have said that you must obey me by following the teachings that I gave you, and by paying attention to the words of my servants, the prophets, whom I have kept on sending to you. You have never obeyed what they said. Jeremiah 26:4b-5 (Twenty-seventh Sunday after Pentecost)

**THE WORLD:**

A toy that comes with a separate sheet of instruction and that needs to be assembled.

---

Part of the fun of a toy like this is that you get to put it together yourself. *(Take the parts from the box. Let the instructions fall to the floor.)* First, you have to figure out which part goes where. Sometimes the pieces don't seem to fit quite right. So you have to make them fit. *(Put several pieces together until you develop a problem.)*

Something is wrong here. All of the pieces came from this box, but they don't seem to go together to make the toy you see on the box.

Sometimes we feel like this toy. We have all of the parts we need for a good life. We have health. We have food and clothing, family and friends, a place to live, a school. We live in a free country. All of these things are parts that make up our lives just as these parts are supposed to make a toy.

But often the parts of our lives don't seem to fit together. We are unhappy or angry. We feel guilty, bored or jealous. Things go wrong in life.

The problem with the airplane was that I didn't follow the instructions. Did you notice this? *(Show the sheet.)*

This shows how all the parts are to be put together. If I follow this, these pieces will make the toy you see on the box.

We often have the same problem when the parts of our lives don't fit together. We aren't following the instructions. Our Bible reading says, "I, the Lord, have said that you must obey me by following the teachings that I gave you, and by paying attention to the words of my servants, the prophets, whom I have kept on sending to you. You have never obeyed what they said."

Jeremiah gave this message from God to people who lived around 2500 years ago. Many prophets had told those people that God would help them. God had promised to come as a Savior to put their lives together for them. But the people didn't listen to the prophets. When they had problems they did not go to God for help. Instead they made their problems worse by putting their lives together the wrong way. They didn't follow the instructions.

Jeremiah's warning also applies to us. Jesus has come. He is our Savior. When he died, he forgave us for putting our lives together the wrong way. When he rose from the dead, he put our lives together the right way. We still have problems. We still wonder if we will turn out the way God promised. But we can trust Jesus. God made us, so he knows what we need. He sent Jesus to be with us. Jesus is a part of our lives; so he knows how to put us back together.

Some people say, "If all else fails, read the instructions." But Jeremiah says, "Read the instructions before you fail. See how God helps us through Jesus our Savior."

# Christic Has Two Jobs

**THE WORD:**

I will give them a king like my servant David to be their one shepherd, and he will take care of them.

Ezekiel 34:23

(Christ the King—Last Sunday after Pentecost)

**THE WORLD:**

A shepherd's crook and a crown (pictures or small replicas may be used)

Adults sometimes aren't sure what they should say to children. So they ask, "What do you want to be when you grow up?" That's a hard question to answer because you've got a choice of a lot of things to become. You may want to do many different things. Or you may not have any idea what kind of work you want to do. Or if you do know what you want to be, you might do that and then become something else. For example, you might be a teacher; then become a principal. Or you might be a factory worker; then become a supervisor. You might start as a salesperson; then be a sales manager.

Our Bible reading tells us about David, for example. His first real job was as a shepherd. *(Show the crook.)* He took care of sheep. He had a crook like this to help him walk where the sheep walked and to help him reach a sheep that needed help. Later David became a king. Then he threw away his shepherd's crook and wore a crown like this. The crown meant he was the one in charge. The crown showed everyone that David was the most important person in the country.

Ezekiel tells us about David the shepherd who became a

king to whom is compared the Messiah that God promised to the people. When Ezekiel wrote these words the people were waiting for the Messiah to come. Now we know that Jesus is the Messiah. When Ezekiel told the Old Testament people what to look for, he also told us what we now have. He tells us that God says, "I will give them a king like my servant David to be their one shepherd, and he will take care of them."

Jesus was to be like David, both a shepherd and a king. But there is a difference. David was a shepherd who became a king. Jesus is both shepherd and king for us at the same time. He wears the crown and he also carries the shepherd's crook.

When Jesus was on earth we saw how he was a shepherd for people. He helped sick people, he was kind to lonely and sad people. He wanted to be with people who needed him. Then we saw how he became a king. He rose from death to show that he had won the battle against sin. He went up to heaven and promised he would come again as a king who would rule over heaven and earth.

But Christ the King who wears the crown still has his shepherd's crook. He still is with the people he loves. As he rules, he also cares. Like some people today, he has two jobs. Both are important to him.

As you decide what you want to be when you grow up, remember you have a shepherd king. Jesus is with you as a king to promise you a life with him forever. He is also with you as a shepherd to help you all the time.